FOXSONG

John Talmadge, first white child born at Lake Arrowhead, pictured on his horse 'Prince' in 1919, at the IS Ranch.

FOXSONG

100 Years of Cow Ranching
in the
San Bernardino Mts. / Mojave Desert

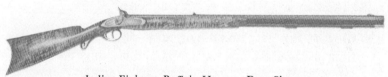

Indian Fighter - Buffalo Hunter - Deer Slayer

by Kendall J. Stone

ISBN 0-930704-26-6
LIBRARY OF CONGRESS CATALOG CARD NUMBER 88-63517

Linotype composition & typographical design by the
SAGEBRUSH PRESS
POST OFFICE BOX 87 . MORONGO VALLEY, CALIF. 92256

This book is for my Darlin'
MARY ROSE LOUISE

Foreword

Kendall J. Stone has been recognized for many things throughout his life.

He is a family man and a gentleman. He was in the First Special Service Force in the European Theatre during World War II.* He served an honorable thirty-year career in the San Bernardino Sheriff's Department, retiring from the position of Undersheriff. His real love and personal satisfaction in life has been to spend every moment possible as a cowboy. Few men have enjoyed life on a ranch as much as Kendall, and few men are as skilled handling horses and cattle.

Being a cowboy, raising and working with horses and cattle came naturally in Kendall's life. He is a direct descendant, fourth generation, of a pioneer cattle ranching family in San Bernardino County.

The pioneer Talmadge family settled in the San Bernardino Mountains in the 1850's. The family operated a logging and lumber mill in the mountains along with their desert and mountain cattle ranch. So as Kendall grew up being a cowboy, a touch of the pioneer was a way of life.

Spending a large amount of time living and working in the pioneer setting gave Kendall the personal experience and knowledge that qualifies him to write about the early years and history of the popular Southern California mountains and desert.

Since retiring from law enforcement, he has dedicated himself to in depth research to add historical facts to his own connection with the past. This commitment to the knowledge of yesteryears will leave a legacy to his children and yours and mine so this special time in history can be reviewed with assurance of accuracy.

I feel deeply privileged to consider myself a personal friend of

---

* The First Special Service Force was a para-ski unit. Kendall also served in the Aleutian Campaign, received a Battlefield Commission in France (1944), and was discharged in 1945 with the rank of Captain.

Kendall Stone, and honored to have known such an exemplary, energetic man who gave me many examples in life to follow, a man I enjoy being with, working in a patrol car or riding some trail looking for wild cows.

FLOYD TIDWELL
Sheriff, San Bernardino Co., Calif.

Contents

Contents

Illustrations

Individual photographs will be found on pages:
52, 61, 67, 79, 84, 91, 97, 109, 118, 126, 132, and 137;
Photographic sections appear between pages:
30-31, 52-53, 84-85, 112-113.

All illustrations are from the author's personal collection.

ᴖᴗ

Foxsong

A charming, uncharacteristically romantic custom of early American woodsmen, mountain men, professional hunters, buffaloers and Indian fighters was to name their muzzle-loading rifles. They did this with imagination, romance and amazingly candid presence of mind, just as though the rifles were members of the family or special close friends, which of course, they were. The name a man gave his gun told much about the man.

Now these hearty, rough individuals, mostly uneducated or with only a small amount of book learning, were not known for being romantic, imaginative and innovative. Yes, but we must remember how close they felt to these rifles. Their lives, their scalps and their families' lives and scalps often depended on the protection given by these weapons, as well as the "bringing home of the bacon," only accomplished by the expert use of the family providers—man and rifle.

Any trip had as its first item of importance the obtaining of sufficient lead, powder, gun tools and spare parts to last at least the duration of the planned move. This meant protection and food, neither obtainable in any other fashion.

Even the women were taught at least how to reload the weapons and to assist their menfolk during Indian and bandit raids.

My great-grandfather, Francis Lebaron Talmadge, had such a gun for many, many years. During the 1850's he fought Indians with it on his drover and covered wagon trips from St. Louis to Sacramento; killed buffalo, deer and antelope to help feed the members of his party; and killed deer in the Little Bear (Lake Arrowhead) areas to help feed his sawmill hands at the Talmadge and Caley Mill in Blue Jay.

With this gun he also fought the last Indian fight in the San Bernardino Mountains, killing at least two Indians in a standoff of several hours between nine or 10 white men and 30 to 40 Indians, on what came to be known as Indian Point, now Hamiltaire. The stalemate came to an abrupt end when he killed the second Indian, who turned out to be the chief of the band and, upon the chief's being shot to death, the other Indians broke and ran and were seen no more in Little Bear.

So, considering the length of time he owned the gun and all the things for protection and food that he did with it, certainly it stands to reason that he felt a close brotherhood with such a weapon, and he, like so many others, named his rifle and treated it like a member of the family.

The name? I'm sure he didn't come by it quickly or easily. It was an important decision, and he came up with "Foxsong," so romantic in sound and conception that I can just barely believe it.

Of course, it was a very special gun—make and calibre long since forgotten. Its unusual feature, especially for the mid-1800's, was that it was a double-barreled rifle, possibly the only one in the San Bernardino County area in those days—and, of course, therein lies the secret of his success as an Indian fighter coming across the continent as well as at the Little Bear fight. Coupled with the fact that he was a crack shot, the double-barrel made the difference.

Most Indians had never seen a double-barreled rifle, and, knowing the length of time it took to reload a muzzle loader, they would peek and peer out from behind a rock or tree and when fired upon knew they had plenty of time to run to another location or, as they frequently did, stand up and laugh and make an obscene gesture at the shooter.

Well, I guess I don't have to go into great detail on how he came to be chosen by the whites as their leader in Indian fights; how he killed any number of Indians, including the Chief at Little Bear; or that he was feared by all Indians who knew him, by contact or reputation.

So there we have a crack team, man and gun. Just as it was true of the U.S. Cavalry, that every place man and horse ventured became part of the United States, so it should not be left unnoticed that many hundreds of man-and-gun combinations on the frontier also occupied and made the United States a safe and livable place for those that followed them.

Was the man-and-gun relationship as important in winning the West as our present day accounts indicate? Or is its importance solely in the present, in the legends we nurture of men and gun and frontier? I wouldn't hazard a guess, but it's undoubted importance in both instances is not to be denied.

Foxsong—indeed! As beautifully romantic as calling a girl "darling."

Chapter Two

ᝣ

Leisure Was Precious During Lumbering Days

The Talmadge and Caley Sawmill in Little Bear was one of the oldest businesses in the San Bernardino Mountains. The very first mill that they had was in the general vicinity of the present dirt dam of Lake Arrowhead.

It was a water-powered mill, not too efficient, but usable. The mill workers could place a log against the saw and go home for lunch; upon their return, the log would almost be sawed through. Better than having to do it all by hand! Soon, however, they obtained one of the modern miracles of that day—a one-lunger donkey engine—and moved that mill site to where Blue Jay is now. It was an efficient, practical and productive mill, cutting thousands upon thousands of board feet of lumber every summer, the mill being closed down in the winter when everyone moved to San Bernardino where the youngsters could attend school.

The three Talmadge Brothers—Will, John, and Frank—were all involved in the mill and lumbering with their father, Francis Lebaron Talmadge.

They were all raised there, and John was born there, the first white child ever born in the area now known as Lake Arrowhead.

During the summer each year (frequently on the Fourth of July), the Talmadge and Caley mill would sponsor a celebration and big dance near the mill site. A big crowd would come up from San Bernardino and other areas and stay for several days.

Prior to the big party, Francis (Frank) Talmadge would have his sons and his mill crew construct a large, raised platform for dancing, and they would smooth up the dancing area as best they could. Music was produced with a minimum of instruments, usually a fiddle or two, a piano brought up for the occasion, and whatever else they could come up with. John Talmadge could "chord" the square dance music on the piano when needed.

15

They frequently danced all night. The San Bernardino mountaineers loved a good time—dancing, eating, and conversing, even a little drinking, just like we do now—and when the infrequent occasions arose to have fun they made the most of it, reliving and talking about it for weeks.

When the celebration was over, they would tear down the dance floor and bandstand and haul it to San Bernardino, along with the other lumber from the mill, so some parts of several of the older homes in San Bernardino could be said to be built, partly, out of romantic, fun-loving square-dance-flavored, pine boards from the Fourth of July celebrations in Little Bear. If some of those houses could talk . . . well, you fill in the blanks. Love, romance, stolen kisses, proposals—each generation thinks they invent all those things, but, really, there is nothing new under the sun, and you can believe that.

The boss was Francis Lebaron, of course. He ran the whole operation. As a form of relaxation and fun he would occasionally ride into Dark Canyon (the present Miller Canyon) with a pack horse, and bring back three or four deer to feed the mill hands. He was never known to fail; he was a dead shot with his old double-barreled muzzle loader "Foxsong", and he enjoyed the outing—his form of relaxation—just as tens of thousands go hunting even to this present day on their vacations and days off.

Also on occasion, he would send one of his sons and another man with two or three pack horses to Fish camp, now known as Snow Valley. They would camp down there for a couple of days and go down into Bear Creek each day and, even while eating all they possibly could, after a couple days both pack horses would be loaded down with trout in the panniers. A layer of moss and leaves and a layer of trout, et cetera, would return to the mill cookshack at Blue Jay, and the trout would be used to help feed the sawmill crew.

In the entire mill operation, the three sons each had a special and important job before they were out of their teens. Will, the oldest, nicknamed "Teet," drove six or eight span of oxen, and dragged the big logs each weighing tons, to the site of the mill. He also moved them two or three at a time to the mill with the same oxen hitched to a large, strong, solid, wooden-wheeled log truck. The catch here was that you had to use the same oxen, by the use of lug chains, to load the logs onto the solid, wooden-wheeled trucks.

Great Uncle Will told me that in some instances, to connect the chains or to move logs only two to six inches to put them in proper position, he would take his wheelers, hitch them to the log, and speak to them to get them to move the log slightly. First, he would position them leaning into the yoke and then with his voice, using no lines or reins on the cattle, he would tell old Broad and Duke to "hunch it," and those fine, trained oxen would shove carefully and instantly into the yoke, moving the huge log a matter of inches, just as they had been told.

Amazing? Yes. Unusual? Not with bull team experts like Will Talmadge to train them (though they were not really bulls). Pretty? He said their response and intelligence were beautiful to behold and appreciate. Necessary? There was nothing else in the woods where they worked capable of moving that weight. Special breed of cattle? Yes, in a way, for it took years to train them; several breeds and mixtures were used, but almost without exception they were "stags" (steers that had been cut late in life and so had a special development of muscle). Also, almost without exception, they weighed up to a ton each.

Strong? Two big, well-trained oxen (one span) could pull as much or more than a horse six-up. In fact, it was common to hook one span onto a six-up with its wagon stuck in mire, and pull horses and wagon out of their dilemma. In those days, it was customary to have a set of bells on each horse team, and when one team had to pull another team out, the bells were relinquished to the team that had helped. During certain rainy seasons it was not unheard of for a two or three span of oxen to have so many bells they had "won" that they could scarcely carry them or find room to hang them.

John, the middle son, known as "Peg" to his contemporaries and as "Puppup" to his grandkids (including me), was involved with the chore of hauling the finished lumber to San Bernardino on a wagon with four or six-up teams of horses. The work horses in those days, the 1870's-1880's, were not large like we have come to think of work horses nowadays. The wheelers might weigh 1,000 pounds or even less, and the leaders 850 to 900 pounds—smaller than most of our saddle horses today.

Up and harnessing his team by 3 a.m., the lumber having been loaded on the night before, Puppup would be on his way down to San Bernardino while it was still dark; this over either the old Mormon Road or the old Daly Road, both impossibly steep, narrow, rough and hazardous. Some places were so steep that the teamsters, John Talmadge and Charlie Martin, had to drag a log behind them for short distances going downhill to keep the loaded wagons from running over the team. Upon returning, they dragged a small log just behind the rear wheels, so when they stopped to air the team on the steep parts, the wagon could roll back a foot or so and wedge against the log. Thus, the team could take the pressure off their collars, rest, and catch their wind in preparation for the next pull. This was especially helpful if the wagons were loaded going back up the mountain.

A round trip took from pre-dawn to dusk, and after returning to the mill they had two more chores to perform. The first was to reload the wagon and the second was to cut a new wooden board brake shoe and install it; they wore out a two-inch brake shoe each trip down and back up. Adding to an already long day, they then had to unharness their teams, tend them, doctor them (if needed), and feed them. The feed was all the natural grass hay they could eat and a 100-pound sack of rolled oats for each team (four or six horses). The horses worked so hard for such long hours they needed that much grain to keep up in flesh—and they were as hard as nails doing that strenuous work six days a week for six months each year.

The hay was cut from the natural mountain grasses that grew in the large, beautiful meadow now located on the bottom of Lake Arrowhead. The mill hands cut hay (grass) up to their waists and forked it onto large farm wagons to be hauled to the barn and stored, cured and salted.

In the winter when the mill was closed down and everyone moved to San Bernardino, the oxen were driven to the Chino Rancho and put on pasture for the winter. The Talmadge ox brand was the ampersand (&) reversed; 40 or 50 years later it became ex-sheriff Jim Stocker's horse brand.

The third and youngest son, Frank, nicknamed "Fish," worked exclusively in the sawmill itself and was in charge of the mill crew and the production of lumber from logs.

One summer they had a tragic accident which happened so quickly it was over before anyone could react. A workman came in late and drunk. He walked up on the platform alongside the big circular saw, lost his balance, fell over on the saw and cut himself completely in two. Suicide? They never were positive. Modern safety measures— guard rails, protective coverings, etc.—were not in use then, and the possibility for such accidents was ever present.

Uncle Frank was the athlete of the family, both as a runner and a baseball player. Baseball was the favorite sport of the men in those days from eight to 80. From ages 10 to 20 particularly, the Talmadge boys played baseball at every opportunity, and played all day. When it became lunchtime, instead of going home to eat and wasting all that good playing time, they would find a field or area where a short green grass known as "pepper grass" grew. All the boys from both teams would lay down on their bellies and eat that tasty, peppery, short grass, just like a bunch of cattle or horses; maybe it was not as good as Mom would have fixed for them, but it left more time for baseball. Pepper grass and a drink out of the creek was lunch.

Chapter Three

ભ્

Will Talmadge Was as Big as His Legend

William Seymore Talmadge was a pioneer, bullwhacker, lumberman, cattleman, fox rancher, amateur biologist, horseman, land subdivider, philanthropist, storyteller and a tough old buzzard, who, the older he got the more he looked like a legendary Indian chief. He was, in fact, 100 percent English.

The oldest son of Francis and Nettie Jane, he was born at "The Monte," now known as El Monte, on March 17, 1862, moved the same year to the San Bernardino Mountains—Little Bear and Blue Jay, to be exact—and lived in the mountains for most of the rest of his life. He died April 11, 1945, at age 83 years and 24 days.

His father was a charter member of Phoenix Masonic Lodge in San Bernardino and Will was raised to the third degree the day he was 21. He was soon followed by both his brothers, John and Frank, into the same lodge. At this writing there are four generations of that family in that lodge.

Will's nickname to his contemporaries was "Teet." He was William to some and Gramps to his grandkids who adored him. (His grandson Bill Betterly is a former county supervisor.)

So many stories abound on so many levels about his physical and mental prowess, that where to begin is difficult and where to end is impossible, but you gotta start and stop someplace.

As a teenager he was so stout that he almost always wrestled two or three other boys at once, and if he only fought one, he kept one hand behind his back. One old-timer many years ago said, "You wouldn't believe the pair of shoulders Teet had, and the strength that went with them."

Once in the early 1880's, a world's champion boxer came to San Bernardino and offered to take on all comers. At first there were no takers, but finally they persuaded Will to put on the gloves and get in the ring with this "champion," who had more than 100 fights to his credit.

They fought for some time. There were no rounds; you just fought until one was down. It was finally stopped—neither hurt nor neither knocked down—called a "draw," and the fighter said of Will when the fight was over, "That man is as strong as any man I ever faced, and to make it worse, I could hit him easily, but I couldn't put him down, and I couldn't erase that smile on his face."

About the time he was in his middle teens, his father put him to hauling and dragging the logs out of the forest with ox teams. In other words, he became a "bullwhacker," although the cattle were not bulls but stags, bulls cut after they are grown and have developed that heavy muscle and extra neck muscles. Each ox weighed approximately one ton, and they drove from six to 10 span. Their strength was awesome, and they did the work that D8 tractors do now.

Those cattle worked all summer in the mountains and spent the winters on the Chino Rancho in pasture (the grass there described as over the top of the cattle's backs).

The cattle became very gentle, very smart and very cagey. When they were turned loose at night to graze, someone had to go get them the next morning and, although they all had bells on, they were very hard to locate because on frequent occasions they would get into the center of one of the patches of willows and when found would all be frozen like statues—they knew they would be hard to find if their bells didn't ring, and the longer they could remain hidden the shorter the work day. And they did that very deliberately—it certainly was not by happenstance.

Will has been heard on many occasions to tell how much smarter cattle are than horses—no comparison, he said. Since he spent his whole life with cattle and horses, and was a man with his thinking cap on all the time, he, beyond any doubt, was right. First proof of this, of course, was that the ox spans had no reins, no lead ropes and no rings in their noses, and all 10 or so span would be completely controlled by voice only—except for a big two-handed bull whip which occasionally chastised an errant ox, and quickly got all his ducks back in a row. They really were smart and knew why and for what they were being whipped.

And, according to William, it was a thing of beauty to see a strung-out 10 span of oxen turning, twisting, pulling, stopping, starting, going right or left, with the bullwhacker at some distance (50 feet or so) and only yelling, but at any rate in total control of those giants. Never touching them, he had their full attention and full compliance with his every verbal command, a thing of beauty and a joy forever to Will Talmadge.

I readily admit he was special to me and I both loved and admired him. He was such a role-model for young men and boys—hard working, strong, masculine, smart, an outdoorsman and willing to answer questions and help any young man who sought his advise or counsel. He was the greatest man to talk to on a one-on-one basis, and his knowledge was phenomenal, even though his education was marginal.

And another small item: of all the three Talmadge brothers, William was the only one with a true sense of humor—the others were pretty typically English in their humor, response to humor and ability to be humorous.

By the 1880's the Talmadge Sawmill in Blue Jay was no more, and Will went into the cattle business in Big Bear and ran his cattle on the Mojave Desert in the winter. He wasn't really a great cowpuncher, didn't rodeo and didn't break colts, and wasn't overly interested in running wild cattle, of which he had a lot, but believed in letting them go if they ran off. "We'll get 'em next spring."

In other words, he was a "thinking man's" cowboy, better known as a "cowman," and owner and operator of a cow ranch. He didn't work for someone else, but was always the ramrod owner, and didn't have or need a foreman. Nowadays they would call him an owner-operator in private enterprise. His was the American way at its very best and most basic and most successful—the fulfillment of the dreams of the millions who came to these shores. Apple pie had to become as American as he.

Another industry akin to Big Bear was "fox ranching," and Will and a partner ran one of the largest fox ranches in the area for many years. From this ranch's fine breeding stock came the famous "Pride of Big Bear," in a distinctive golden-platinum fur developed here.

Will was more than just an outdoorsman, though he was that too; but his knowledge of the flora and fauna of the San Bernardinos and the Mojave was great, and unexpected unless you really knew the man, and then it was only typical of a man so removed from the ordinary.

A true story of his patience, knowledge, know-how and ranch expertise was his habit on a bad, dry spring—when many of the cattle were poor and weak and hardly able to make it to the high meadows—of coaxing his whole drive, his whole herd, into the mountains without loss, even though the cattle might be literally dying on their feet and other ranches would be losing stock. His method: slow and easy, don't hurry an old poor cow with a young calf. He would talk to them, get off his horse and walk behind them up the steep places, often letting the rest of the herd go on up the trail and out of sight. If the old cow insisted on lying down, he just sat in the shade of a pinion and talked to her a little, then after a half hour or so he would go over, tail her up and slowly, sometimes oh-so-slowly, he would follow along.

Late that afternoon, about dusk, the rest of us, already in camp and unsaddled and eating, would see this old white-faced, long-horned, poor, slow cow and her little half-starved calf coming up the trail out of Rattlesnake Canyon. He would walk her by the corral and the other cattle and by the camp and start her down the trail toward Arrastre Creek where she could get a drink and a bellyful of grass, then come back and care for his horse and then himself.

Not very Western and exciting? I guess not, but he was probably hands-down the best cowman that ever ran cattle in Big Bear. Nowadays, with roads, trucks, baled hay, special supplement blocks and all, the cattle don't face such starvation and hard times, but they did then—and also it took a cowman and cowboys to run a ranch in those days. Now? A dude and a jeep loaded with hay, pulling a horse trailer with a pampered horse in it, think of themselves as the last of the Wild West. Further deponent sayeth not.

On top of all of that he was a very public spirited member of the Big Bear Chamber of Commerce ever since there had been one. He often gave a beef, barbecued it and served it for the chamber on the Fourth of July. Gave several acres of land for road development, ramrodded the big (at that time) project to remove the stumps and trees from the lake. Most people here now don't know that the dam when new covered up acres of forest and trees that had not been removed. Will stacked and burned them, to beautify the lake and the shores. He also gave of his time and money to assist in blue-stoning the lake. All his work at no expense to anyone, as civic-minded in his way as any resident of Big Bear.

Through his second wife, Betsy, he also heavily assisted the local Women's Club. His first wife was a Rathbun. Ring a bell? Rathbun Creek is out of Moonridge. Her parents were some of the original cattle people of Big Bear and among the first owners of the upper IS Ranch (now Moonridge). In fact, the upper IS Ranch was Will's home (exact location just above present zoo) for many years; and Moonridge at that time, up to and including most of the 1920's was the most beautiful area in the San Bernardinos, and he was one of the men who appreciated living in beauty.

So you see, he not only looked an Indian, he had some of their characteristics, i.e., living in beauty, and human enough to know you shouldn't judge a man till you have walked a mile in his moccasins. Tolerance is what his English forebears called it.

An amusing story my granddad John used to tell on his big brother Will was that when young, and prior to getting married and having a home of their own, they both, along with other members of the saw-mill crew, slept in the bunk house. He said that everyone was unhappy with Will because he was yelling at the top of his lungs all night long! Still driving those bull teams he had been working with all day, calling them by name (Broad and Duke were his two big leaders), he was driving them, hooking onto logs, dragging them down toward the solid wooden-wheeled trucks or to the mill yard. He just about drove everyone else out of their minds.

His brother said further that this was a common fault with bull-whackers in general. They yelled at their charges all day and they yelled at them all night as well—and, subsequently, kept everyone awake. Since Will was bigger, older, tougher and stronger than the rest of them, they were afraid to wake him up and tell him to shut up.

Will always rode a top horse, particularly good at traveling and cutting cattle, not as so-called "cutting horses" do now, but slowly, carefully—never riling up the herd, and never running or jousting off even an ounce of fat. (That's where the profit is on a ranch.) Besides, a real cowman (and they always were few and far between) never ran or even trotted cattle if he could manage to keep them walking slowly.

When Will took over the IS herd, way back when, the cattle were multi-colored, wild and most had never seen a man off his horse —and whereas the little calves being branded nowadays just get back on their feet and walk away from the fire, formerly in the late 1800's and early 1900's almost every calf would leap up when released, bawl, shake his head and charge a man or horse if in front of him. They meant it in spades, and scattered the ground crew and fire tenders, and sometimes ran right through the branding fire and scattered ashes, branding irons, woodpile and sheep dip in every direction.

Will spoke on several occasions of being able to remember being put in a log cabin at Blue Jay in 1867 with all the rest of the kids and women and a couple of men to guard them, while the rest of the available manpower (eight or 10) went out to meet 40 to 50 Paiute Indians that were marauding in the area and had already injured one white man and burned one cabin, near the head of Dark Canyon. They met them and fought with them for several hours on Indian Point (now named Hamiltaire) and killed one or two and drove them off. One man named Welty received a shoulder wound from a spent bullet, and Will remembered seeing his father drawing a silk handkerchief through the wound to remove any cloth or impurities that may have lodged there.

As an aside, the Indians were not well armed, but neither were the white men all that well armed. One had only an axe and one a pitchfork, though the rest all had good muzzle-loaders and, typical of most of those old pioneers, knew how to handle them.

William S. Talmadge, quiet, reticent, low key and unassuming, had so many friends no one could count them. When his two sons, Otis and Willy, drowned in Big Bear Lake in 1909 there were more than 600 mourners at the funerals in San Bernardino, and 600 was probably a large percentage of the population of that day.

One last yarn to tell about Will Talmadge: almost more so than any other person known to any of us, he was practically impervious to either heat or cold. This may be a little thing but added measurably to his reputation for being tougher than anyone in the mountains. When he went downtown to San Bernardino as a boy the town kids would yell, "Here comes Will Talmadge. He's been up in the mountains getting stout!"

When he was 65 or 70 years old he again proved his imperviousness to cold. At the Pipes Ranch there was an eight-inch cement pipeline coming from a sunken dam and weir box in the canyon about one-half mile above the house, and the takeoff for the cement line was in the bottom of the weir box in about six to eight feet of cold water. The water came right out of the rocks and bedrock. Every couple of years the willow roots would grow into and almost stop up the pipeline, and the stoppage had to be pulled out by hand. Frequently the roots ran 20 to 30 feet down the pipe and its removal was difficult.

On this year, several young cowboys, including Bill Betterly, Roscoe Cline and Bud Waite, all tried to go down into the water and unplug the pipeline, but due to the cold could not stay under water long enough to accomplish this. So William took off all his clothes but his long johns and, laughing at those young men, went into the water, dove to the pipe outlet, pulled the root plug and 20 or more feet of attached roots out and brought it up with him as he came back up out of the water. "Tough old buzzard," was one of the repeatable left-handed compliments that was heard that day and not infrequently when that subject came up for many years. That water, like the big spring in Moonridge, was so cold it felt like it was freezing your teeth when you took a big drink. You had to slow down and drink a few swallows at a time.

To ride in a cold, blowing snowstorm with him was an education in humility. He didn't shiver, he didn't turn up his collar, he didn't turn blue with the rest of us, and on the hottest Mojave Desert summer day, riding after cattle when it was 120°, he still wore the same long johns he wore in the winter. Claimed they absorbed the sweat, dried off from any little stirring of air and kept him cool.

Not many care to try long johns when working in the Mojave Desert in summer. Afraid they'd likely melt. And it is too bad but his imperviousness to pain, heat, cold, thirst and hunger is probably not inheritable—or at least it is skipping a couple of generations; just ask "Wild Bill" Betterly, to whom "Gramps" was a truly great man. I couldn't agree more.

Having known Will Talmadge all my life, I have been aware because of my relationship with Will and John Talmadge, Will Rogers, Frank Bland, General Fredricks and a very few others (you'd have several fingers left) that you don't have to be president or king to be a "great man." As a matter of fact, most presidents and kings and generals are not. But such "great" men stand out from the crowd like white on black in whatever walk of life they may be found, and neither being educated nor rich has anything to do with it. Is that quite a statement? I suspect it is, but I also have a gut suspicion it is true.

We Americans have drifted into a destructive psychology of assuming that people who don't have a lot of money are somehow unworthy of recognition or high office. And, just as destructive, we are inclined to look up to and even honor those with wealth—even when it is inherited and not even "earned the old-fashioned way." A misleading and sad state of affairs and such a false front is detrimental to the general welfare of the nation as a whole. Wasted and unused talents are a loss we, nor any other society, can ill afford.

An example? One man was very successful as a soldier, a politician and a president of the United States, but a total loss as a businessman trying to make money. Who? Harry ("The Buck Stops Here") Truman.

William had the knack of asking the right people the right questions and not forgetting what he learned. He knew the common name, the Indian name and the scientific name of almost all the grasses and chaparral and trees in the San Bernardino Mountains and the surrounding foothills and desert. His knowledge extended to the area of knowing whether the grass was edible and fattening, what browse and bush the cattle would eat and what type lumber or wood came from the different trees of the area, along with the names (common and scientific) of mountain and desert flowers and to which family each belonged.

Along about the time Will Talmadge was in his 70's the Great Depression came along. That and other things sometimes got him pensive, down in the mouth and worried about money, his family, the cattle, and the general running of a huge cattle ranch when there was no money flow anywhere. At such times he often went to the Whitewater Ranch winter headquarters and spent a few days checking on the cattle in that area and the farming part of that headquarters. On more than one occasion he made the remark that he could be in front of the old cement block house and look up and south at the beautiful rugged mountainside and peak of San Jacinto (Tahquitz to the Indians) —and that relaxing and looking at that huge, beautiful, one-of-a-kind mountain would drain all the tension and troubles and worries and woes right out of him. He almost conversed with that old mountain, and I can vouch for the fact that he and it were friends and totally *sympatico* with each other. Very few white men have had that enviable association with nature, but he did. And I'm sure many Indians have such feelings and attachments; you have got to be pretty down to earth.

He noticed, appreciated and understood nature to a degree unknown to even exist by most people then and now. Interesting course and class in nature, both plant and animal, just to ride horseback with him, say, from Big Bear to Yucca Valley. It took most of the day and he would point out places of interest, the arrastre in Rattlesnake Canyon at the cottonwoods, the smelter below Bill Kramer's place, the spot where an Indian's body was found.

He'd discuss the yearly rainfall and where and when and in what amounts the moisture had to come to bring on the spring grass, to make a good pinon year, to leave enough dry, standing feed in the fall to winter the cattle through in good shape.

He'd explain how to, from up on the mountains (Tip Top was a favorite place) look down over the desert and be able to see where the summer thundershowers had crossed so as to be able to take advantage of this extra fall feed. He also pointed out, remarked on and discussed the various grasses, flowers, browse, cactus and particularly poisonous plants (some only poisonous in certain stages of growth, i.e., lupine).

He had so much knowledge and he did his best to pass it on, and did so in many instances. However, most did not have his retention, and surely much or most of it was lost.

An exciting, interesting, many-faceted bullwhacker, cattleman, fox farmer, storyteller, nature lover, horseman, lumberman, amateur philosopher and, better than most, botanist, he could easily be referred to as "Mr. Big Bear Valley." No man, living or dead, lived here longer nor was any more influential in its history, its times, its progress and its advancement over a period of 80 some years; from practically a total wilderness to a thriving resort area, from an almost negative population to a citizenry of thousands.

Much local mountain history went down to oblivion with the passing of William Seymore Talmadge.

Chapter Four

ои

Bill Knick: Real-Life Paul Bunyan

On June 10, 1869, in the state of Pennsylvania, a full-blooded Seneca woman gave birth to a boy baby, and that day became a date of historical significance to Big Bear Valley. Indeed, it was a red-letter day, for that baby, whose father was Dutch, was named William Edwin Knickerbocker. He was later better known to his friends and contemporaries in the San Bernardino Mountains as "Bill Knick".

Knickerbocker was an early settler, master woodsman, and a dead shot. He could saw up, saw down, or chop down more trees by hand than any man who ever lived in the San Bernardinos. Rugged? You wouldn't even believe the stories of his physical strength, endurance and energy.

When still a boy in Pennsylvania, he worked in sawmills as well as in the woods, getting logs for the mills. His mother had 20 children, six of them Knickerbockers. Along about this time, and knowing that she was dying, she deliberately walked into the surrounding woods and disappeared, never to be found. Such reasoning may be strange to us, but her motives and actions can hardly be questioned by those of us who are now, and were then, almost totally ignorant of that culture.

Bill Knick and his brother, Ed, headed for Arizona at the time of the land rush which produced the Sooners in Oklahoma. At that time there was a smallpox epidemic in the West, and they sent for and received doses of smallpox serum, which they administered to themselves.

Ed was a mining engineer, and the brothers got into mining in Arizona. Not striking it rich, they came on to California, Ed arriving first. In 1901, Bill came to Big Bear, and the two took up mining claims in Holcomb Valley, and apparently lived at Doble.

In 1904, Bill married Rose Anna Pollard. The children of this union were Ellen, Gertrude, Marjory, Harold, Katherine, and Florence. The last of this clan, Florence, was born in 1920. Gertrude died young and was buried in Redlands. Katherine also died young, and was buried in Van Duzen Canyon. (There was a marker for each of these girls in the Doble Cemetery, but neither were actually buried there.)

Bill mined in Holcomb, hauled water to Rose Mine when it was in operation, and hauled by horse and wagon big logs to a Banning sawmill via Victorville. Then in 1914, he became the Big Bear Lake dam keeper, and lived at the old stone house above the dam on the south side. He wintered there by himself, Rose Anna spending the winters in Redlands so the girls could go to school.

In the 1920's Bill built the now-famous, historic log mansion on Knickerbocker Road. Pennsylvania Avenue, which bordered Knick's property, was named by him after the state in which he had been born, and for which he had fond memories.

Bill Knickerbocker's prowess with both axe and saw is legendary, and still inspires awe, admiration and argument among the men in Big Bear who are most familiar with the use of such tools. Stories abound, and have been told and retold, both before and after Bill's death. These stories originated from other than Bill or his family, and the truth of them is unquestioned among all who knew and worked with Bill at the time.

One story relates to Bill's strength and durability. When he lived at the dam, he bought his meat at Walter Warren's IS Ranch store. One day he purchased a quarter beef and, throwing it up onto his shoulder, started walking back to the dam. A quarter beef can weigh just about anything, but it is almost certain that he was carrying 100 or more pounds. About halfway to the dam, or just west of Boulder Bay, he met a carload of friends and stopped to talk for about 20 or 30 minutes. He did not bother to put the beef down, and as his friends drove on toward Pine Knot, he turned and walked on to the dam. The total walk from the IS was three-and-a-half to four miles, and he never took the weight off his shoulder until he hung the beef up at the dam house where he lived.

Another time, in the 1930's, Bill was a Civilian Conservation corps foreman for a bunch of young men aged 18 to 25. His assignment was to build a trail from Holcomb to Lucerne through country that is steep, dirty, and full of rattlesnakes. He and his crew had constructed a good, zig-zagging trail, and were more than halfway to Lucerne when he began a game that would expand his legend.

When the work day was about over, he would order his crew to take their tools and canteens and head back up the trail to the trucks. After they left, he would get the lay of the land for the next day's trail construction, and in about 15 minutes or so would pick up his tools and canteen and start up the trail.

In a little while, he would catch up with a laggard and hurry him up by taking his canteen. A bit farther up, he would take another boy's brush axe to enable him to hurry on up the trail. The upshot of it all was that Bill would be first to reach the truck, carrying a half dozen tools (axes, brush axes, etc.) and about ten canteens. Then he would stand there and laugh at those pooped-out kids who were trying to stay with him coming up the trail. And he was in his 60's.

Another time, when Bill Knick was 84-years-old, he decided to chop down a "big" pine tree to prove he could still do same, and he chose one of the big old monarchs. This was one of those which were so large that the first sawmills in the mountains couldn't handle them, the type seen on postcards, or the kind of old giants that the swallows return to each year. These are the biggest trees in the mountains.

At any rate, Bill started chopping with his axe which was always sharp enough to shave with, and he chopped that huge pine down to the ground and never stopped or rested one single time. Though there are at least 20 times as many people there now as in that day, probably no man living in the San Bernardino Mountains today could even come close to duplicating that feat, no matter what his age.

Now there was a man! Must have been some kind of a magic mixture —half Seneca and half Dutch.

The truth of the matter is, Paul Bunyan was a piker. And Bill didn't even have a blue ox. Bill Knick was indeed our own, well-remembered version of Paul Bunyan. Of him can be truthfully said, "A man is a man is a man".

Francis Lebaron Talmadge at (approx.) age 25, owner of Foxsong, with which he provided food for numerous wagon-trains that traveled from St. Louis to Sacramento in the 1850's. Later, he owned and operated a sawmill at Little Bear (Lake Arrowhead).

The Talmadge home at Little Bear as it appeared in the 1880's. The site, now under 150 feet of Lake Arrowhead water, was the birthplace of John Talmadge in 1864.

Hauling lumber from Little Bear to San Bernardino during the 1870's. John Talmadge and Billy Martin are the teamsters.

The Talmadge sawmill in Little Bear, sometime in the 1870's. The many people present—obviously not laborers—are visitors from the lowlands of San Bernardino and Los Angeles, up to the mountain country for a picnic. The meadow in background is now at the bottom of Lake Arrowhead.

Francis Lebaron Talmadge as he appeared in the 1870's. He was the father of John Talmadge and the author's great

The legendary Bill Knick with his hunting dogs 'Ranger' and 'Major'. The locale is near Big Bear Dam, probably

Six yoke of oxen, belonging to Will Talmadge, seen moving huge logs to the mill at Little Bear. Note the solid wooden wheels and gut chain holding logs on wagon truck. Each ox averaged about one ton in weight.

Mrs Martha Whitby (seated) and daughters (l. to r.):

Wm Talmadge on 'Old Blue' bedecked in fancy parade

Chapter Five

When Ridin' & Ropin' Were for Real

Four large cattle ranches formerly used the San Bernardino Mountains as their summer ranges, all bringing their herds into the high pastures approximately the first of May, midway through Spring. In the fall (October or November) the cattle were driven back to their winter ranges on the Mojave Desert. It usually took most of a month, in the Spring, to get all the cattle on top of the mountain.

Riding, gathering, driving, cooking over a campfire and sleeping on the ground, cowboys fought heat and wind and dust on the desert and cold and snow frequently, that early in the year, at Rose Mine and Baldwin Lake.

Old-time cattlemen were conservative and conservation minded and never deliberately harmed, over grazed, or damaged their holdings —they believed wholeheartedly in "two grasses per cow and never two cows per grass."

It stands to reason that they were careful of all things to do with the improvement and care of their ranges; for example, fighting erosion, experimenting with new browse and grasses, and building dams and irrigation ditches. In the four ranches there were many miles of irrigation ditches, mostly unused and gone now; and opening seeps up to become springs where a few sections of pipe and a water trough for the cattle as well as for deer, dove, quail, chukars and all other game and varmits. They had not insulted or spoiled any of the range in the 100 years they had been running cattle here—and were not about to start, because they meant to be here for another hundred.

There were then, and there are now, some people—some eggheads, some government agencies, and some pseudo, nouveau-conservationists —who blame the cattlemen and their charges for denuding the mountains and desert of much flora and fauna. That is simply not true, but some still believe it and espouse the idea to this date. If you want to see damage to flora, fauna and watersheds, you might observe the practice and results of four-wheeler, motorcycle and dune-buggy damage in both the mountains and desert, what lumbering activity does to small trees, as well as denuded ski slopes and watershed damage that occurs at casual and careless development in the high country as well as the lower arid regions. At any rate, I think anyone can agree the harm caused by ranchers and cattle pales to insignificance in any comparison.

Also we have fires now that burn homes, watersheds and other property—as well as people—because the policing of the forests, brushland and watershed is generally not vigorous and forcefully pursued.

Other occupants in other days and other times were more apt. The Indians burned sections of the mountains for who-knows-how many years, while the Spaniards and sheepmen systematically burnt the mountains off every fall as they left the high country with their large flocks. (Many thousands of sheep summered throughout the San Bernardino Mountains long before cattlemen arrived.) They, with studied deliberation, set fires behind themselves every fall as they returned their flocks to the Valley below.

So what's the point? Merely showing that with controlled burning, along with thousands and thousands of sheep and/or cattle to eat up the explosive yearly tinder (grass), the fires were much less likely to spread over thousands of acres and much less likely to burn up the big timber. The short fuel was eaten and the brush and chaparral were burned before they got six feet high, creating the type of fuel that now burns everything in its path, including part of the north end of San Bernardino, which occurred as recently as the early 1980's.

I am aware that many residents and vacationers have various objections to cattle running in the mountain areas, but the choice is apparent —cattle (or sheep) or hundreds of thousands of acres of burnt off brushland with no pines, cedars or other big trees that make the mountains what they are.

Is that overall too simple an aswer? Probably. But surely the problem must be faced. Throwing millions of dollars at the problem (more men, more equipment, more airplanes, more choppers, et cetera) cannot be the final or ultimate answer. There have to be better ways, that are also cheaper on the taxpayer. Hopefully several approaches can and should be made. They are using grazing animals for this purpose even now in some places. And back-fires and controlled burning take both courage and expertise, but are being used to some extent in fire hazard areas.

Many of the big old pines used to have one side burned and scarred (often from lightning strikes) but no real or permanent damage to the tree resulted, and this in turn provided a bonus to the old-timers and early settlers with an enending supply of tasty and everlasting "pitch-gum". Far superior to commercial and modern sugarless gum, this natural kind was probably full of vitamins and minerals, and for sure did no damage to the teeth; in the long run it probably did a lot of good. Also it did not contain any additives, coloring, artificial flavoring, salt, harsh nitrates or other chemicals that seem to be in all our food these days.

Very few of the present resident, visitors, skiers or vacationers have tried real pitch-gum or even know what it is. Amber jewelry is a first cousin to pitch gum—the only difference is a few million years.

Anyway, as a cattleman and horseman (as well as outdoorsman, hunter and tracker) who was bred, born and raised here, I couldn't help but throw in the foregoing on the things of nature. It's long past time that someone should speak out about the problem, the cause and the results of the same. And let the people who are presently in charge of such things know that we of the public applaud their efforts to stabilize and protect our forest and other flora and fauna with methods known to be effective for hundreds of years.

Having been born here, I am proud to relate that my family, several generations ago, arrived in the San Bernardino Mountains in the 1850's, and by 1880 were running cattle in Big Bear. And of the stories I heard first and second hand from those people about lumbering, cattle ranching, mining, fox ranching and starting the first subdivision in Big Bear, were classic regional lore, some of which I will attempt to incorporate in the pages of the book the reader is holding.

I digress here—in fact, I digress so much I'm not sure anyone but myself knows when I am digressing and when I'm covering the subject, but be that as it may, I have noticed a compulsive tendency of persons new to the Valley, to change the names of area ranches, lakes, et cetera, from their old pioneer, long-estblished names to more insignificant, meaningless names. Most old-time names were justly earned, therefore are meaningful, not fabricated from fanciful thinking.

Some examples of name changes? OK, try these: Little Bear—now Lake Arrowhead; Upper Old Ranch—now Moonridge; Dead Man's Lake—now Lake William; El Pinon Rancho—now Camp Oaks; Pine Knot—now Big Bear Lake City; China Gardens—now Interlaken.

I note also Moonridge Country Club of which the golf course is still there, but the clubhouse is gone; and Bear Creek Store, now just a turnout on Highwest 18 west of the dam. The very beautiful, green, verdant little town of Cedar Springs—now under Lake Silverwood. And what was formerly a beautiful meadow and then a green, beautiful golf course with little Oriental bridges and huge standout pines, is now the unsightly, blacktopped area known as Big Bear Airport.

Chapter Six

ໝ

Rodear!

The busiest, most interesting time of year on the ranch was now. The activities that resulted in the cattle being moved from their desert winter range to the high summer meadows began sometime in April each year. A fencing crew would be sent to check and repair the fences of the corrals and fields at the Devil's Garden, Morongo Valley, Warren's Well, the Pipes, Bains Ranch, Rose Mine, Shay's, China Garden and the IS Ranch horse meadows, and it always turned out to be a week or 10 days of hard work.

At approximately the same time, one or two cowboys would go to the Whitewater Ranch where the drive began and where the remuda was kept during the winter months (except for few head kept for use at the various winter cow camps), and at this time of year these horses had to be gotten up, shod up and doctored where needed. Their feed was cut down, but they were put on hard alfalfa or barley hay to help get rid of the soft filaree bellies they all sported. And frequently their long-inactive soft winter backs would be bathed daily with a heavy solution of water and salt to harden them up and help prevent saddle sores on the hot, long (10-15 hour) days they had ahead of them on the big gather and move to the cool, fattening mountain meadows some many uphill miles away.

Almost every step from Whitewater to Big Bear was uphill, some of it narrow, steep, rocky, slick and dangerous. Several head were lost every few years from falls from the steeper, rougher sections such as

Toutain Canyon, as well as some losses in bog holes and quicksand, particularly in Shay's Meadows on Baldwin Lake. But with the fences fixed, the bogs marked, the worst of the trail made better and the horses shod, doctored and hardened up, the day was fast approaching to get every man and horse, the chuck wagon and cook, a freshly killed beef and all the myriads of items, tools and grub together like ducks in a row, and the rodear was ready to actually begin moving cattle.

Up to now you had time to change dates, rest a day, alter plans, argue strategy and so forth, but as of the first moving of cattle on the first day of gathering there was no stopping, changing, resting, turning back or indecision allowed or possible. The ranch and all of its resources—men, horses, cattle, equipment—were committed, and nothing stopped day or night till all were at least on Baldwin Lake where a short breather could be taken before the next step.

And so, very early in the morning of a day in the middle of April, for all the days now would be early to late (with even some chores, moves, repairs and minor changes made at night), the wheels started turning, and the ramrod over a three-to-four-day gather from Whitewater Ranch would send mounted crews to Palm Springs, One Horse, Snow Creek, the Morongo Indian Reservation, Gold Canyon, Whitewater Canyon and all places in between to track down, gather and drive all cattle to be found to the pasture at Whitewater Ranch. Here in the afternoon of probably the fourth day would be about 450 to 500 head of cattle and about 100 spring calves, some not 24 hours old yet.

Practically every night one or more calves would be born, all the way to Big Bear. Many times the old mother cow would be left with her new calf to come on at her own pace. Many caught up at the next two- or three-day stop, and the others usually arrived on Baldwin Lake within a week or so. This method gave the pretty little white-faced calves a chance to lie down and rest whenever they pooped out on the long, uphill climb (better for the cow, better for the calf) and showed the ranch was run by a cowman. This part of the gather was moved late in the afternoon across the highway and up the hill to the corral on the Devil's Garden.

After a dry camp that night, early the next morning the cattle would move well and cover the ground to the water at Mission Creek in good shape. That's really the only good thing about a dry camp—the next morning the cattle will travel instead of trying to stop and feed.

Before noon we stopped the herd to drink and rest an hour or so on Mission Creek and try to wait for the outriders, who had been sent to check Desert Hot Springs and Mission Creek, to catch up to us with any cattle they may have found.

Then the long, slow, hot afternoon going up the Dry Morongo. This was a bad few miles for everyone, but the little calves would be "laughing" (panting with their tongues out) at you almost at once. It was soft sand, it was uphill and it was hot, and it would take all afternoon to get over the hill and into Morongo Valley and drive across to the corral for the night. All afternoon the little calves would be sneaking off behind a bush to lay down and hide in the shade, or they and their mothers would be trying to go back.

Some of the time that was a rough, wishing-it-was-over kind of afternoon. But as always, this too shall pass, and by the time the cattle were in the corral, the big cattle had gotten a good drink of water, the calves had all sucked their mothers, the sun had gone down, the temperature had dropped, the cook came up with a cool drink of water, a hot drink of coffee, and a big platter of steaks, and the horses had been grained and fed a big flake of hay, and all of a sudden everyone, cattle, horses and men (even baby calves) realized the world was a pretty fine place after all. The trials and tribulations of the day were forgotten.

But even so, by the time the cowboys finished their canned peaches, smoked a cigarette and stood around the campfire about 15 minutes they were all ready for bed and rolled out their bedrolls and climbed in. Soon a little snoring, the chomping of the horses, the stirring around of the cattle and an occasional coyote yip was all that was to be heard. And thus ended the first full day of the drive.

So far one steer had been killed falling off a cliff in Toutain Canyon, four calves had been born, the cook almost cut a finger off getting steaks off a half a beef in the chuck wagon, three rattlesnakes and a sidewinder had been killed, and beards, bad breath and body odor were already beginning to grow.

But so what—we wouldn't see a half dozen people from here to Big Bear, and the crew were all in the same boat so no one thought anything of it. In those days girlfriends of cowboys described them as always having chapped lips and smelling like a horse, and despite the utter truth of such statements, cowboys always had the prettiest girls in the county. Married 'em too—where do you think cowboys come from?

And you can believe it—after a cowboy becomes a truck driver, a movie star, a developer, a sheriff, a promoter, a politician, a tramp, a millionaire or one of the heads of industry, he will fondly remember his years as a "hand" as the best of his life, and is prouder of the title "cowpuncher" than any other job.

Just remember: to make that statement absolutely true, we are here talking about cowboys, not dudes. I'm talking about those who have been in dust, blood, dirt, sweat and cowshit up to their armpits, not those whose roughest ride was on a soda fountain stool.

Hey—let's not get lost. It's just breaking day, steak, eggs, biscuits, fried spuds and coffee are all down, the horses are fed and saddled and it is just light enough to tell a cow from a bush. So the ramrod orders several hands to gather the mouths of the upper and lower Big Morongo canyons, the upper and lower Little Morongo canyons, and the valley proper as we move the herd through. For the rest, open the gate and get the herd untracked and strung-out. We got a long ways to go today.

Big old herd bulls and dry cows lining out, heading for Warren's Well, they know exactly where to go and how to get there. The problem is keeping the wet cows and little calves in the drag up with those leaders who only need to be held up a little from time to time. Even so, the herd is spread out for about a mile.

So the whole day is spent moving the herd up to Yucca Valley, receiving little bunches of cattle here and there that the outriders have located and brought in, killing one big mad coontail (rattlesnake) who almost struck a baby calf who had curiously sniffed at him, pushing the cattle off the dirt road and letting the two cars by (the only ones we saw all day), and ribbing each other on who was going to get to ride Nevada (an outlaw) in the next day or so. We knew he had been caught up out of the wild bunch a few days before to be used in order to let a couple of other horses get a day's rest at some point on the drive.

Uphill most of the way, and hot all the way, but we finally, about 4 p.m., put the herd, now about 600 head, into the field at Warren's Well. Be here gathering about three days. There was a good adobe house, stove, running water and good corrals and barn for the horses, one of the better campsites for the drive. One hundred sixty fenced acres with the feed saved all spring to keep the herd happy while we gather. Several old beds and springs in the house and barn so most everyone got off the ground for these two or three nights.

Up early all three days and gathered about another 100 head and

25 to 30 calves from Coyote Hole, Black Rock, the Tanks, the Covingtons, Smith Canyon and Quail Springs in what is now the Joshua Tree National Monument. Pretty routine, but several cowboys went to the square dance at the old rock schoolhouse in Yucca. Nevada gave the man assigned to ride him a fit, as usual, almost bucked him off twice and, as always, he was harder to catch in a box stall than an ordinary bronc in a 10-acre field.

Oh yeah—one of the hands went home with a pretty widow from the square dance, didn't get in till 4 a.m. Don't know what happened, but he sure was hung over all day, wasn't worth a damn. A good thing Nevada wasn't assigned to him that day. And the owner of the ranch came within an ace of giving him his time; don't care how much you drink or how much fun you have, just so you are on tap and able to put in a decent day's work. Most cowboys tough it out better than that guy did.

Early next morning with a yet bigger herd, the ramrod directed the drive up Sand Canyon to Water Canyon and headed across the black brush bench where Pioneertown is now located, enroute to the Pipes. Outriders were responsible to gather Bullshit Spring area and Chuparosa—and we, of course, picked up everything that the drive happened onto. About 3 p.m. the herd was in the Pipes Ranch field (about 200 acres). By then the herd had grown even larger.

The Pipes Ranch gathering area was fairly large, and for three days the Pipes Valley, Pipes Canyon, Pipes Windmill, Painted Rock and Reche's Well areas were gathered and all the cattle located thrown into the Pipes Ranch field with the growing herd. Almost every morning the growing, lowing, bellowing, fighting cattle in the big herd would attract a small bunch of cattle to the outside of the field where, when we discovered them, were promptly put into the field to assure that they would go with us when we left for the next day's drive.

The last places gathered into the Pipes were Painted Rock and Saddle Rock Springs. When they were denuded of their little bunches of cows and calves, preparations were made to pull out and head the thousand plus cattle to the Rose Mill.

This would be a long day, probably the longest and toughest of all, with Sticky Hill and the Needle's Eye right in the middle of it, so a good early start was necessary. Most of the hands worked to push and guide the cattle up the trail, knowing it would be dark when we got to Rose Mine, even though this was almost the longest day of the year. But a couple of riders were sent, long before the sun came up, to go up onto Duncan Flat to gather what they could from Ruby, Longhorn and Wood canyons, as well as Burro Flats, and to hurry as much as possible and meet the drive in Antelope Valley. There we would hold up, bed the cattle down briefly in an attempt to let them get to us. It usually worked; when it did not they were late, tired and hungry by the time they got to the Rose.

It was a small, dry corral and for some reason especially spooky to the cattle. They were always on edge and disturbed on that night of the drive, and, sure enough, about midnight a coyote sang and they stampeded back down Rattlesnake Canyon. Instantly everyone was hurrying, cussing, trying to get saddled; it was an exciting melee around there for a few minutes. One of the young colts, a three-year-old, got so shook he broke loose and ran off into the night, and but for a good moon it would have been twice as bad.

But finally (actually only five minutes) several were ready and mounting, half dressed. With only half their gear on, only one cinch tightened, breast collar flapping, shirttails snapping in the breeze, a half dozen cowboys headed back down the trail into Rattlesnake Canyon where a high, thick, long string of dust could be seen in the canyon ahead of them, running hell bent for leather back down the trail, having to run up on the side hill frequently to go around many old gentle cows who already had enough of that foolishness.

All this in the dim moonlight in the bottom of a steep, dark canyon, was some kind of a test for the surefootedness of those desert/mountain rough-country horses. And they again, as many times before, proved their worth and safely carried their riders, wide open, with the pedal to the metal, down that canyon, passing cattle all the time in an effort to get in front of the leaders, circle them and bring things to a halt. And the sooner the better, because as Rose Mine corral was a dry camp, no matter where they stopped they had to return to Rose Mine and then immediately go on to Baldwin Lake. That was a long day anyway you looked at it.

The fastest horses and riders got around the leaders about a mile and a half past Bill Kramer's Sleepy Hollow Canyon. After stopping their forward motion and getting them to mill around so the other cattle would be absorbed into the idled herd when they arrived, the men would then resaddle their horses, straighten their saddle blankets, tuck in their shirttails and wonder how many hours would pass before they got back to the Rose and some coffee and breakfast.

The sun was coming up now. The cattle didn't want to go back up the canyon. Most cows and calves had become separated and they were making such a din, bawling for each other, that you couldn't hear yourself think. The horses were hot, tired, thirsty and hungry—all in all it was not a very auspicious beginning to the last day of the drive to Baldwin Lake. But no matter what, Baldwin Lake was where you had to be by evening.

After a half hour or so they had about half the herd, and those still coming were just walking and were calmed down so they started back up Rattlesnake—but they had help they hadn't counted on. Several of the other riders had counted to about 500, or half the herd, and when they passed that many they turned the leaders of that back half around and took them to Rose Mine corral, so at least they didn't have to drive and pick up the whole 1,000 head. With this help all, or almost all, were back in the corral by 10:30 a.m. and the corral was patched up where they ran through it.

Tired and hot, most of the herd lay down in the shade of the pinons and were happy to rest.

Breakfast and coffee never tasted so good. Horses got grained too. During the conversation around the campfire while we ate steak and eggs, one cowboy had an interesting tale to tell.

Seems he was running down a little ridge in the almost-dark, trying to pass the stampeding cattle when, without warning or apparent reason, his horse set up very sharply, almost sending the rider over his head. As he came to a complete stop, the cowboy could hear, in the deep silence of that side hill, the rocks that the horse had kicked ahead of him, as he came to a panic stop, bouncing off the walls of a mine shaft as they fell. And this, when he got a good look, was only two or three feet in front of his horse. The shaft, about five feet by five feet, was over 30 feet deep when examined by several cowboys who thought they were being "spoofed." But the tracks and the shaft were as described, and he was one lucky cowboy to have been riding an alert equine athlete that night.

With some haste because of the time of day, the cattle were put on the trail to Baldwin Lake. After stopping briefly at Arrastre Creek to let those who had not watered in Rattlesnake slake their thirst, the herd was pushed on to Baldwin Lake and got there while the sun was still up.

Camped that night at Shay's Ranch, and it was evident that cattle, horses and men had put in a big tiring day—horses were fed extra heavy, bedrolls were filled early and not a soul stirred till morning. Then, bright and early, the cook being his usual obnoxious self, rolled everyone out at 5 a.m.

That's not bad. Many people get up at 5 a.m., but very few then work till 6 or 7 at night. It didn't pay much, work was hard, hours long, but it is the greatest way of life in the whole world—ask any ranch cowboy or cattleman.

Still lots of work to be done, and spent that next day separating out the beef steers and driving them to the China Garden and Moonridge where they would be left for the summer to gain weight and get fat and go to market about September 1.

A couple of welcome days of rest for man and horse and then all the cows and calves on Baldwin Lake were gathered. In about two big days 300 head of calves were branded, ear-marked, bulls were castrated, all were vaccinated for black leg and finally turned back out on Baldwin Lake.

A few days later, after the bull (now steer) calves had had a chance to heal up a little, a large number of cows, calves, bulls and yearlings were driven to the Narrows and Grout Bay, Juniper Meadow, Bluff Lake, Merriam Meadows, Metcalf Bay, and located for the summer.

With that kind of feed, the cows gave lots of milk and the calves grew big and sassy and by fall many weighed as much as 500 pounds. That's big, but that's what mountain meadow grass can do. For instance, the steers in the China Gardens gained close to as much per day as cattle in a professional feed yard. There were cattle scales, first near the present airport and then moved to the China Garden, and the cattlemen would weight several head at intervals all summer to keep track of the weight gain, and it was surprising even to them.

And now it all had to be done again, always some strays left during the first rodear and it was necessary to go back for them on a second drive—although seldom went further back than the Morongos.

Starting there, every waterhole, trough, stream and windmill had to be checked for cattle sign. The cattle had to be tracked out and driven back up the same trail as before. This drive usually took only about 10 days. We usually stayed at the Pipes and normally gathered less than 100 head, but when this drive was over cattle were pretty scarce on the desert range. Sometimes a half dozen or so would summer on the desert but never very many—and it was usually on this second drive that you located some of the few wild, or orahana, cattle that occasionally cropped up.

This made the second drive very interesting. A few big runs after wild cattle could be counted on, and catching them, leading them out and handling them are what kept a cowboy's interest up. It's not only fun, it's dangerous, it's outdoors, it's men among men, it's good horseflesh proving itself. It's all the skills of a horse and rider used at one time—one of the few places where horseflesh is called on to run wide open in rough, rocky, steep, brushy country, then build to something and rope and handle it, tie it up or down and later lead out a big steer or orahana bull about the same weight as your horse, sometimes heavier, then handle him again to get the rope off.

So your horse runs full out in bad country, jumps big logs and down timber, jumps wide ditches and gullies, jumps off three- to five-foot banks on the run, then jumps up onto banks near that size, puts you up close for a loop after running maybe several miles and then stops and holds the animal, who is probably charging, and fight him—tell me about some other jobs of horses, anywhere, where they are asked that much of, frequently over and over. Never heard of any other equine job that was so demanding or dangerous, ever, nor even close to it. Almost all other horse jobs and skills are on level, smooth, soft surfaces—therein lies the big difference.

Even endurance rides, while admittedly tough, are all on trails. I don't know any other job where you occasionally run the shoes right off your horse and run the horn-toe coverings off the cattle, leaving them running on the bloody ends. At no other job is a horse asked to do so much—and good cowhorses do it with gusto.

After about six weeks or so of long days and hard work there comes a period now in parts of May and June when everything slows down—ride easy through the cattle every day or so to keep tab on them, start a colt or two, kill a beef for the ranch consumption, start taking strips off a wet, pliable hide to start the makings of a riata, re-shoe most of the horses, haul a load of hay up from Whitewater and just generally take a breather and try to put a rein and a stop on the just started colts. And we settle down to enjoying the summer weather and bring a big bouquet of lemon lilies to the prettiest girls in the world, go several nights a week to Stillwells; accept, enjoy, host and put up numerous friends and relations who also come to Big Bear to enjoy the most wonderful summer climate in the world.

Cookouts, barbecues, boating, fishing, horseback rides up to the ridge above Bluff Lake to watch the boats traveling both directions between Catalina Island and the coast. Took many people there who didn't believe you could actually see the ships, and always came back down the trail via Castle Rock, from the top of which is another spectacular view of Big Bear Valley. There were no houses or roads between Boulder Bay and Metcalf Bay in those days, and the return ride along the lakeshore was another beautiful experience, long remembered by those fortunate to have been there and seen it during the years when it was at its most spectacular.

Cowboys do not fall in love with horses, but respect them more and care for them better, and work as equal partners with them daily, on a much greater scale than most of those who do. The facets of it are unknown to most horse owners, but the rapport between a good hand and a top horse is a beautiful thing to see—all of us talk fondly and spin yarns of remembrance about old cowhorses who have been dead for 20 to 50 years. "Remember old Spelick?, why once I saw him . . ." "Yeah, and remember how little old Chief used to . . ." "How about Nevada? Now there was a horse as notorious as Al Capone—and just as dangerous." "And good old Snip; now there was a rough-country cowhorse and the best horse Bob Hitchcock ever rode." "One-eyed Moze could run farther, had more wind and bottom than any two horses ordinarily had." And a story worth reading could be written about all of them, plus many more. True working relationships existed between such horses and cowboys who eagerly did more than their share of the work just to prove that they could.

These were some kind of outstanding equine partners—Ace, Eleck, Old Blue, Buddy, Dick, Chub, Prince—you could cut cattle on old Prince with nothing more than a loop on his nose. These and many more known personally by the author in the last 60 years, were a part of a disappearing breed.

There are fewer and fewer ranches left each year where such horses are bred, broke, trained and ridden. There are still some areas where such horses continue to work, but ranches too have become modern, progressive and mechanized. Airplanes, Jeeps, motorcycles and even helicopters now, in many areas, do much of the cowponies' work.

I guess maybe that's the saddest statement I've ever seen in print. But men on equines working bovines will continue to be the most romantic aspect of this and several other countries as long as life exists on this planet. Can you imagine books, poems, movies, plays and children's games without a lasso, horses and cowboys?

Chapter Seven

ᐯᐱ

"I S" Brand

The Talmadge Bros. Company use of the IS brand was begun by Will Talmadge in the 1880's. He took in his brothers, John and Frank, as partners, then they bought out Jim Smart, Felipe Curoz, and others.

Felipe Curoz did not have very much schooling (maybe none), and when he sold out he had his cowboys pass his cattle, one at a time, in front of him and the Talmadge buyers, where they were given into keeping of the IS Ranch hands. As each cow, calf, steer, heifer or bull was driven in front of Curoz, the buyers would hand him a $20 bill; he figured everything was worth exactly $20 and in this way no one could cheat him and he knew just where he stood. Felipe subsequently bought a saloon on the east side of D Street just north of Third Street in San Bernardino and stayed there and in that business for the rest of his life.

Their summer mountain range and pastures included what is now Moonridge, which at that time was known as the Upper IS Ranch. The house, barns, corrals and killing pens were located near, slightly easterly, of where the horse rental stables are now situated. There were no roads, no fences, no houses and no people in those days, except for the ranch headquarters. Although now, with all the "progress" and "improvements" it looks battered and bruised, those of us privileged to see it in the 1920's and before remember it as one large meadow from the top of Moonridge almost to the China Gardens, with a couple hundred cattle spread out all over it. It was indeed a magnificent and gorgeous picture, so different from now. That was the San Bernardino Mountains at its very best.

The beef fattening pasture was the China Gardens (where the Safeway supermarket is today*) and where Chinese grew truck for

---

*The iron hand of progress continues on, and even Safeway could not avoid it this time. In 1988 the local branch of this supermarket chain was engineered out of the picture (at least in name) by corporate manipulation.

44

the miners in Holcomb. You can now look at that once-beautiful meadow and see only subdivisions, stores, banks, drug stores, flood control ditches, paved roads, parking lots and much more "progress" to which I again, tongue in cheek, allude.

Talmadge Bros. also ran cattle from the head of the lake to Gray's Landing on the North Shore, including the Minnelusa pasture, where the ranger station, houses, paved roads and signs have largely obliterated its beauty from sight. That little meadow which ran from the lake to approximately one-quarter mile behind the ranger station was an example of a beautiful mountain extravaganza, which is now barely recognizable. They also ran the South Shore from Eagle Point to Boulder Bay, and here at Metcalf was the second of the IS Ranch headquarters. Walter Warren's store, Will and John Talmadges' homes, a barn and horse pastures were also located here.

Walter Warren's store was doubly famous for the meat market he ran as part of his enterprise. The IS Ranch killed two or three beefs each week for the store and people came from Los Angeles, San Bernardino and many other places to buy his meat. It was grass-fattened beef that had never been frozen, shipped or chemically treated nor fattened on hormones. When you flapped a lip over a big steak from Walter's store, you were enjoying beefsteak at its very best, both tender and flavorful. The myth of corn-fed beef was only foisted onto the American housewife when it became necessary to do something with the huge over-abundance of corn. The flavor is not as good as grass-fattened. It is, however, considerably more expensive. The only apparent difference is that the fat on grass-fattened beef is slightly yellow, and on corn-fed beef it's white. What's the difference? About 30 to 50 cents per pound.

Another area where the IS cattle ran was Merriman Meadows and Bluff Lake. It was a favored area to put the mother cows to raise big, fat, well-fed calves, and thousands of IS calves got their start in the Bluff Lake area. It was in that part of the ranch I can remember my grandfather, John Talmadge, stopping, when we were on the way home, getting off old Prince and gathering an armload of lemon lilies and taking them to my grandmother, Martha Levinia, because she was so into flowers, especially lemon lilies. They are so fragrant and sweet you have to put a large bouquet out of the house at night. There are still lemon lilies in that sector, and they are rare and protected, but can be enjoyed by the persevering flora seeker in damp green spots and deep canyons.

The winter range for the IS was the Pipes Ranch, Pipes Valley, Pipes Canyon, Pipes Windmill, Reche's Windmill and Giant Rock area. Also Warren's Well (now Yucca Valley), Black Rock, Covington Flats, Morongo Valley, the Devil's Garden, Whitewater Ranch, Snow Creek and One Horse. Sometimes cattle strayed to Palm Springs, Thousand Palms, and Desert Hot Springs and, of course, had to be rounded up and driven back to Whitewater Ranch.

Among your former Big Bear neighbors on the IS, besides the owners, were the following cowboys: Bob Belt, Bud Waite, Joe O'Rourke, Bill Betterley, Jesse Bangle, Harve Martin, and silversmith and horse breaker Frankie Paul, a former U.S. cavalryman in the Philippines. (An aside—Harve Martin mentioned above is rumored to have ridden with the wild bunch of the Younger brothers in Missouri and the Missouri Breaks when he was a young buckaroo.) The Talmadges and the above mentioned hands broke, trained and cowboyed such top horses as: Spelick, Pinto, Arkansaw, Buddy, Old Blue, Monte, Eleck, Baroso, Pedro, et cetera.

A story could be written about every cowboy and cow-horse mentioned above. Each have anecdotes and backgrounds and histories that cry out to be told and thus recorded and not lost for all time. These men and horses are a part and parcel of the early history of Bear Valley and the surrounding Mojave Desert from Victorville to Banning.

These ranch owners and cowhands were contemporaries with and friends and neighbors of such Bear Valley stalwarts and pioneers as the Knights, Bill Knickerbocker and old Jim Erwin. All old timers had a great mutual respect for each other, did not always agree, but did respect the life, work and moral values of each other.

Bill Knickerbocker once told me that my grandfather (John Talmadge) was one of the "ablest" men he ever knew, and you can rest assured that was the highest type of praise—because to know your occupation better than the next fellow and to work hard at it was an important goal in itself to those of that generation. Paper shufflers, ne'er-do-wells, the lazy, the untruthful, the undependable and the dishonest were looked down on with scorn, and pitied by these stalwart pioneers of yesterday who one and all believed in integrity, hard work and the whipping post.

The year Jim Erwin was 102, he was snowed in at his one-room cabin on Erwin Lake. The local merchants wanted to send him a side of bacon, some coffee and other staples. I was captain of the Sheriff's

Office at that time, and wanting to check on Jim anyway, I offered to snowshoe in with the groceries and did so. He was properly grateful and spent an hour talking and telling me some of his past interesting history. About the time I was leaving to snowshoe back he said goodbye and remarked, "Thank those fine people for me, but will you tell them the next time they want to be so neighborly that I'm old enough to drink whiskey!"

Chapter Eight

ᗡᏧᗣ

September Cattle Drives: the Long, Dusty Trail to Market

The IS Ranch, along with all the other San Bernardino Mountain ranches, sold its beef cattle in the fall, mostly close to the first of September. The majority of the beef steers (two to four-year olds) would be in the fattening meadows on each ranch, and along about Sept. 1 the butcher in San Bernardino or Los Angeles would be called to come to Big Bear to look at and bid on the cattle ready for market. The buyer would be taken by horseback to look at the cattle to be sold. Frequently, along with the steers, a few old dry cows would be offered for sale, and occasionally several old bulls would also go.

This was the day for dickering, horsetrading and the give-and-take fun of each; butcher and cowman, trying to outguess the other on price, cut and deal. It was very important for the ranch owner, this being his only income, so it was also financially serious business.

That day or at least in the next few days the butcher would be there to watch the cattle being weighed. Several "cuts" meant that the steers were not all sold at the same price, and of course the old cows brought their lesser price and the old bulls brought their bologna price.

Very early the next morning (3 a.m.) all hands were up and on horseback by 4:30, and heading for the holding field where all the sold cattle were being held. Just as soon as it was light enough to see the cattle (the days were getting shorter and the nights colder, with ice and frost frequently very much in evidence), the gates would be opened and the beef drive to Victorville and the Rancho Verde would be underway—down the north shore of Big Bear to Fawnskin, turn north to Fawnskin Meadows, Hanna Flats, cross Holcomb Creek, pass Big Pine Flats and put the cattle on the Coxey Ranger Station meadow for the first night's stop. It was a long, hard day; cattle, horses and men were ready for a big drink of water, chow down and rest and sleep til 3 a.m.

The drive was carefully orchestrated and the beef cattle handled as carefully as possible so they did not walk or run off any more fat than necessary. They worked under a standard four percent shrink anyway, figuring this was about what the long two-day drive and 12-hour railroad journey would take off of them between Big Bear and the Los Angeles stockyards.

Three a.m.—Yup, and the cook would be up slamming pots and pans and being thoroughly obnoxious about getting everyone up. Then grain the horses and eat breakfast (steak, eggs, biscuits, fried potatoes and coffee), saddle up and again as soon as you could see, turn them out and head down the hill from Coxey to the desert; this after the standard warning by the ramrod to hold up the lead and not let them get to trotting in the downhill road. The whole herd (250 to 400 head) would all try to run, and that was exactly what you didn't want to happen to the beef on the way to market. All downhill to the desert floor, then turn west at about Dead Man's Point and head to the Rancho Verde where the railroad and the loading and holding scales were situated.

And if we were real lucky and had been living right we would see, someplace coming across the desert, the automobile of Gwen Bear. Right then the cattle would be stopped, allowed to bush up in the shade of some yuccas and rest for an hour, while all hands would ride over to eat ice cold watermelon that Gwen would bring out to meet the herd, leaving her famous dude ranch just in time to meet us and I swear save our lives. Never tasted anything so good and so cold.

All good things have to come to an end and we soon roused the herd and drove on to Rancho Verde. The railroad cars would be setting on the siding with the first one positioned and ready to load. As soon as the cattle had drank, they were driven into the corrals and the loading would begin—hot, dirty, splintery work it was, too! Lots of yelling and prodding and cussin', but in a couple of hours all would be loaded and the cattle train would pull out, leaving the whole crew in a kind of lonesome vacuum—no cows, no noise, nothing to do—it really was a letdown.

Looking back a half-mile across the lush green meadows of the Verde we could see the chuck wagon setting up camp right next to a beautiful bubbling artesian well. Didn't take long to get there, spread out your bedroll under some big old cottonwoods, get a big drink of that clear, cool artesian water and then just lie down on the bedrolls, talk, lie, spin yarns, cool off and watch the cook finish up making supper.

Soon stuffed and soon dark; everyone turned in. This, too had been a long, tedious, hot, dusty, trying day, and sleep came easy. Yes, and dawn came early, not 3 a.m., but bright and early everyone was at breakfast. One person horseback would be chosen to follow the remuda back to the IS barn in Big Bear. (The author was lucky enough to be chosen to help once, and go it alone on two other occasions.) Several hands would assist in getting the horses out the gate at the upper end of the Verde (i.e., Bear Valley Road) and there the horses were all released and given a big "hooda". Old Pinto and Long John—to whom this was old hat—would take the lead at a run and gallop, and although sometimes slowing to a trot, would never stop this side of Coxey Ranger Station. If the rider were lucky enough to have caught up by then, there he would catch another horse to ride on to the IS.

Off again, the loose horses would grab a bite of grass, run and trot and never again hardly stop all the way to Fawnskin. The rider was pressed to keep up, and from Fawnskin to the IS horse pasture and barn it was almost a horse race up around the head of the lake and then going west to home—all at a run. It was a very exciting trip for a young cowboy who, however, was well pooped out by the time he got there. Big day in the saddle. But a more glorious way to spend a day (running, horseback for nine or 10 hours) has never been invented.

One year about 1925, John Talmadge was helping Will Shay with his gathering for the butcher and subsequently his weighing of the beef. It seems the butcher was very aggravating and Will Shay, who had a very short fuse, was really fuming by the time the weighing started. It seems this butcher choused and ran and moved the cattle around the corral for three hours, and on top of all that weight loss, he argued over every one-half cent cut in the price till every cowman there was aware of his motive (to make the cattle lose weight, so that he would profit when they went across the scales). Everyone was pretty hot under the collar at this unorthodox and unfair treatment. Will Shay was just about to explode over it. Short fuse, as I said.

They finally got around to the weighing, hours after it should have begun, and each cut, (six, eight or ten head) that was driven onto the scales to be weighed was watched by IS Ranch owner John Talmadge, neighbor and brother-in-law to Will Shay. He, being around on the back side of the scales, was out of sight to almost everyone, and he stepped up onto the scales with each cut. The result was, that aggravating, conniving butcher bought John's 165 pounds with each weighing, amounting to maybe almost 5,000 pounds, and just about what those approximately 250 big steers lost due to the chousing. Poetic justice! At least those cattlemen thought so, and so do I.

Chapter Nine

ᗡᗠ

After Fall Cattle Drive, Cowboys Came Back for Stragglers

The fattening, selling, weighing and shipping are over and it is only Sept. 15. For the next month, maybe more, it is a slack time for ranching. Pull everything in a little closer preparatory to gathering everything and returning it to the desert for the winter.

During the ideal fall you waited for the second snow. Before the first snow you could hardly drive those old cows out of the mountains, they just weren't ready to go—but after the first snow and accompanying cold weather, many of the old native cattle left for the desert on their own.

By the time of the usually-much-colder second snow, the cattle were all ready for the warm desert and were easy to line out on the trail to Rose Mine and onto the desert beyond. Some would be left in Rattlesnake and Antelope Valley, a larger herd would be scattered in the Pipes, Reche's Well, Yucca Valley area, and the last few hundred would be taken to Whitewater Ranch, some located at Snow Creek, One Horse Spring and on other sections north of the highway that the IS owned at that time.

Many times one or two cowboys at Pipes Ranch, Warren's Well, or Whitewater Ranch would keep a couple of horses each to ride in the wintertime. The rest of the horses are released in the desert field and on alfalfa stubble at Whitewater Ranch. And most of the good, old, well-bred Hereford bulls are also placed on alfalfa stubble at Whitewater, so they will be fat and in the best possible breeding condition, come the next Spring. Poor, unready, uncared-for bulls can knock your calf percentage in the head and cost the ranch thousands of dollars. Here we are talking about the little calves that weren't there; they surely are the very ones that do not make you any money.

Now it is necessary for three or four hands to return to Big Bear Valley and pick up the few remaining stragglers that were missed on the first drive. Usually 15 to 30 head are found from Bluff Lake to Baldwin Lake and driven to the desert for the winter. Several expensive tragedies occured when cattle, not found, stayed in too long and were stranded in the deep snow and deep cold. At Bluff Lake one year in the 1920's, eight head of cattle—cows, calves and yearlings—were trapped by the heavy snow in a large willow patch. The next Spring they were found, all dead of course, starved and emaciated; the deep cold of that high territory (more than 7,000 feet) took its toll.

Where they were found two things stood out. They had eaten that patch of willows down to the size of your wrist and gnawed the bark off the big branches right to the ground, and eaten pine cones and pine needles right into the dirt. Secondly, the offal was eight inches to a foot deep, showing exactly the perimeter of the area they had kept stomped out by their presence and movement. None survived, and for years it was a place shown to many ranchers, cowboys and also others as an object lesson on what can happen when you fail to religiously gather and find everything on that second drive out of the high country each late fall.

Again, in the 1930's, just outside the easterly gate of the holding corral at Rose Mine, a few (maybe five to eight) head were trapped in the harsh winter snow of that season (around 1933), and, although they survived, the unquestionable evidence of their long imprisonment and plight was easy to see. The same two things were evident. First they had eaten chemise brush right to the ground and all the dry hanging leaves of three yuccas, gnawed the bark right down to the inner tree itself, ate the pinon bark off, and all the cones and needles were obvious by their absence. They too revealed their exact area in which they were trapped because here too the offal was deep, noticeable and showed exactly the size of their cell.

Now these cattle escaped—but they, like other cattle so trapped, when located the next Spring, had long hair on their bodies and hair three to four inches long on their bellies, and did not shed off properly and normally all the next summer. Though it is hard to describe, when picked up they were wild, skittish, foolish and stupid; trotted with a high unnatural step; acted goofy; and to put it bluntly, were half-witted like the inmates of an insane asylum. Crazy, scared of their own kind, wild-eyed, glassy-eyed, frankly they can now also be likened to human beings high on marijuana or coke; totally self-made inferior individuals, some of whom never come out of it. Just as modern day users (as I likened them to above), they thought they were doing fine but they were skinny, nervous, unreliable, hard to get along with and in some instances dangerous to turn your back on.

Those mentioned survivors from Rose Mine were about as valuable to the ranch as human users of marijuana, coke, horse, et cetera, are to our society. A dreadful indictment of our times.

Kendall Stone on 'Baroso' at Warren's Well (Yucca Valley) in 1938.

The three Talmadge Brothers and their wives (l. to r.): John and Martha, Frank and Maybelle, Will and Wilamina, at Moonridge around 1910. Each lady is holding a bouquet of wild mountain lemon lilies.

Lake Arrowhead pioneers sometime during the 1890's, near the Talmadge mill. Included in the group are: Francis Talmadge, John & Martha Talmadge, Will & Sarah Shay, Burt Talmadge, Myrtle Shay, and Wynn & Cliff Shay. Unfortunately time has taken those who could properly identify each person.

What is now the corner of Big Bear Blvd. and Tulip Lane was once the summer headquarters of the IS Ranch. This is what that site looked like when the pace was a bit slower than these later times of the 20th century. Pictured here are Walter Warren's store, the Buzzard's Roost, milk house, Will Talmadge's house and John Talmadge's log home.

Shay womenfolk brought lunch to the Shay Ranch crew on beef weighing and selling day. The former location of the cattle scales is near present-day Big Bear Airport.

A branding session in full swing at Shay's Corral, with Baldwin Lake in the background. Busy at work are (left to right): Buttons Dean, Dan Withrow and Tommy Davis.

Old-time cattlemen of Big Bear country at a 1927 Moonridge gathering. They are (l. to r.): Cliff Shay, Dale Gentry, Harry

Chapter Ten

ᏜᎾᎮᏗ

Railroad Summit Standoff

Once upon a time, along about 1933, an unusual occurrence happened near the railroad community of Summit, Calif., located at the top of Cajon Pass up from San Bernardino. Seems that for several days the Mexican families who comprised the section crew for that piece of roadbed could, in the quiet of the night, hear dogs barking almost all night long. Being curious, the crew hands noted that their own dogs—as well as neighborhood strays—came in groups of two, three or four, several times a day, drank at the railroad station, laid around in the shade a little while, and then disappeared again.

Mexican people, for the most part, are very aware of livestock—be it wildlife, domestic dogs and cats, etc.—and somehow they surmised that the recent behavior of all these dogs boded ill for someone or something. Knowing that the Talmadge Brothers owned and ran all the cattle in that whole area—from Cajon to the Sawtooth Mountains, and from Crestline to Hesperia—they sent word to the Los Flores Ranch via "Old Pete" who drove the model "T" school bus from Summit to the Los Flores one-room, eight-grade, ten-student school. When the Ranch got word of the dogs' behavior and the section hands' suspicions, John Talmadge, Roscoe Cline, Slim Spence and another hand or two all took either a rifle or a shotgun, and drove in the Ranch's model "A" truck to the Summit. From there the direction of travel of the dogs was pointed out to them, and after proceeding a half-mile southwest across the road and up onto the ridge, they could hear the barking dogs. Spreading out, they advanced in a ragged line toward the noise.

After a short walk they all stopped. Looking ahead of them about sixty yards through the chaparral, they could see about ten head of cattle (cows, calves and steers) bunched up tightly and surrounded by some eight dogs—four or five big German Shepherd types and three or four little feists. The cattle were drawn, wild-eyed and standing in a

53

small tromped out area hounded by the dogs, who had worn a circular trail two inches deep and four inches wide. As the men watched, the dogs were constantly moving around and around the cattle, barking and intimidating these bovine who, it was now realized, had been in this position and condition a minimum of four to five days. Obviously, the canines' eventual victory was only a day or so away, unless the cows and calves received outside help. The age-old battle between the herbivore against the carnivore was being enacted right before their eyes, and just as wolves had surrounded deer and elk and other split-hooved animals for eons, here it was happening in exact duplication in the relative modern day of 1933.

An interesting situation, but obviously only one action was open to these cattlemen. They glanced at each other, and in silent agreement advanced slowly and quietly; the closer they got, the more brush they passed and the better vision they obtained. They reached within 30 yards before one big German Shepherd spotted them, barked a warning, got the instant attention of all the pack (obviously all that barking is more than just a lot of noise) at which point they all turned and ran. The shooting was instantaneous and at least half of the dogs were killed, and those that escaped never harassed any other cattle.

The cattle? They broke and ran, as best they could, down the ridge and into Summit Valley, headed down the canyon in the deep chaparral en route to the Ranch headquarters, and were seen the next day on Hawes meadow. There was a dramatic change in their appearance even that soon; it was obvious they would be 100% recovered within a few days.

Just as it is the truth that the dogs were only doing what comes naturally, then we must admit that the cattle owners too were doing exactly the same. We can do no other than to realize that man has been the difference, and has been the victor in all such meetings for thousands of years.

There is one thing to be noted about the dogs who organized that project near Summit. They, both big and small, had kept the cattle immoble for days, taking turns going for water and rest, but always leaving enough strength at the scene to keep the cattle frenzied and surrounded. All the wolf, dingo, and wild canine blood and cunning came out in these "pets". It's there in all domestic dogs, but is seen only infrequently.

Chapter Eleven

ono

Calves Born Hooked

About 1935 it was decided some 100 more mother cows were needed to add to the Los Flores herd, this coming about during a policy change in which more emphasis was placed on home-grown calves.

To implement this new direction of growth Uncle Frank Talmadge went to Arizona to purchase the new cattle and ship them via railroad to the Los Flores. In a week or so he telegraphed the time and date they would arrive at the Summit railroad station where cattle corrals were available to load and unload.

The cows arrived at the scheduled time, were unloaded and driven down Summit Valley to the Los Flores Ranch. There they were placed in the river bottom field to hold for a few days 'til they could be branded, earmarked, doctored where necessary and checked for ticks or fleas.

The unloading, driving and re-gathering required about three days and in branding and handling them it became more and more clear to Will and John Talmadge that many, indeed most, of these cows were loco, some quite severe while others were only moderately affected. There was nothing that could be done at this point but turn them out on the winter range that ran from Hesperia to the Los Flores and from Summit to the Mojave River.

They did not come with calves by their sides, but the seller had assured Uncle Frank that the cows were all bred and would calve in the Spring. The new season came and these new cows began dropping calves right along with the natives; these seemed a little small but that did not surprise the ranchhands.

But two months later, when the cattle from the winter range were being gathered to take into the Ranch and eventually up into the summer range that ran from Rock Camp to the Cajon Pass and from Crestline to the Los Flores, including Cleghorn Mt. and Canyon, the cattlemen were surprised. Believe it or not many of the calves were impossible to gather with their mothers and be driven to the Ranch. In case after case, when you jumped or startled the cow, the calf ran blindly off in any which direction and did not return, and if you attempted to turn him with a horse he would run into or under the horse and only end up further and further from the cow.

A little study of the problem led to the decision, without fanfare or hesitation, to rope the calves, take them to the cows, and release them close by. This was a good guess and worked like magic—when roped, dragged around a little, thrown within sight of the cow and started in her direction, he would go to her. She, either driven by a second puncher or responding to his bawling when roped, would be easily placed near the calf.

But the amazing thing was, after that treatment, they walked, trotted, ran or stood right against their mothers, and you could not separate them even if you tried—it just took one such lesson, but it entailed roping about 70 calves in the canyon and brush between the Hesperia Airport (which was not there in those days) and the Los Flores outer fence. A lot of good roping practice, but it did slow down the gather for several days. However, never again was there any trouble with those independent spirited calves, and as time went on both the cows and calves became rational and blended into the native cattle with no trouble. And, as best could be seen, the next Spring, calves of those Arizona cows were normal as any other.

You read about children of human females that are borned hooked on heroin or cocaine, and almost for sure those calves were born hooked. The cows, then being out of the country where they had gone loco, got it out of their systems and their next Spring calves were, or seemed, perfectly normal and were noticeably bigger. Might be some kind of an object lesson there for women of childbearing years who plan on having children. Smaller and hooked shouldn't be their objective.

ováo

Cowboy Golf: Early Enthusiasts Fought Range Wars with Cattle

Down through the history of the game of golf, cattle have been mightily attracted to the grassy fairways and the lush, damp greens. And this propensity held true for the Big Bear golf courses at Peter Pan and Moonridge. Really the two are not compatible and should not be together; one does not compliment the other—and a certain conflict is inevitable.

Back in the 1930's the IS Ranch would get frequent calls in the early morning from the caretakers of the Moonridge Golf Course to please come and remove the cattle from the course. In keeping with the good neighbor policy of the Talmadge Brothers, one or more cowhands would be sent on horseback to chase the errant bovines back down to the China Gardens and the dry lake bottom.

Now you have to remember that the golf course slopes quite sharply toward Big Bear Lake, and on these cold crisp mornings the cattle, upon seeing a horse and rider, would head downhill and buck and run and play and spar with one another en route to the lake shore (about a mile away). In doing so they would inevitably cross a green or two which usually had had a sprinkler on it during the night. Of course, their hoofs would sink in from two to six inches while crossing the damp green areas so carefully tended—and the horse tracks did similar damage, because some of the time it was necessary to ride or even run a horse across the tender greens. Well, that did leave holes in the soft greens—however, it always seemed to us that to put 30 or 40 more holes in the green (they already had one with a stick and a flag in it) we were really doing the golfers and the duffers a favor. All they had to do was get their ball on the green, and the chances for a hole-in-one or a birdie were very good, with all those added opportunities.

But we had some rather heated conversations with the greens keepers and even some of the golfers, but they failed utterly in every instance to see the humorous side of the situation. They very pointedly inform-

ed us of the cost and time and effort it took to repair such damage.
Seems they had to spend most of the rest of the day hauling sand and
dirt to fill the holes, removing the green plugs as best they could to be
put back over the filled holes, and combing, patting and tamping each
hole (footstep) back into shape. They even threatened to send a bill
or sue—but never did.

And, too, they never understood that cowmen thought the addition
of a few head of cattle greatly improved its rather stark, uninhabited
appearance. Although unknown to a few, the addition of a few head
of cattle enhances almost any locale, including parks, playing fields,
lawns, gardens, and alfalfa fields, though some people just refuse to
admit it. Poor sports, of course, with no sense of beauty or balance.

It helped the problem not a bit that the IS Ranch had just recently
sold the Upper Old Ranch (Moonridge) to land developers who put
in the clubhouse, the golf course, roads and improvements, and were
happily selling off lots in the area. The old IS cows were pretty ignorant and didn't know about this change and because they, their mothers,
grandmothers and great-grandmothers, ad infinitum, had spent their
summers on the lush green meadows of the Upper Old Ranch, they
continued to automatically migrate there each spring with their new
little calves. They were only too happy to see even more lush, green,
fresh spring grass than usual on the fairway and greens areas. And
they did feel put upon when driven off the very meadows where their
ancestors had dwelt each summer for almost 100 years. The dispos-
sessed Indian tribes couldn't have felt any more cheated.

Of course, many of the same things were happening at Peter Pan
Golf Course; the cattle frequently were found on the greens as well,
with much the same results as at Moonridge.

Despite genuine efforts by the cattlemen to keep the cattle away
and genuine efforts to keep the course management happy, it became
kind of a Mexican standoff. Cow pies left here and there on both the
fairways and the greens were also mightily frowned upon by both
management and players. We were of the opinion that we should be
recompensed for the fertilizer, an idea that really never took hold in
golfing circles.

Finally, the golf course personnel found the situation intolerable,
in terms of the cost in time, labor and money to repair particularly
the greens. One night they managed to drive a bunch of cattle into
an old unused chainlink deer pen that sat between the golf course and
the clubhouse. They then requested compensation for damages before

they would release the cattle. They were feeding and watering the cattle, who were in no way being hurt by a few days in the old deer pen that must have enclosed a couple acres.

This didn't set too well with the cattlemen, since they had no intention of buying their own cattle. After a few days of verbal gymnastics which produced no answers that suited both sides, an action to free the cattle was put into motion by the ranchers. They figured that the area had been a cow ranch for about 100 years and a golf course for a very few, and more or less expected those cattle to go there to graze as their ancestors had.

Anyway, two cowhands—who knows which ones?—at midnight rode over to the edge of the timber just south of the deer pen. One, having a large white sheet tightly folded, handed his reins to the other who stayed put. The man with the sheet walked down to the edge of the pen and climbed over into the pen itself and quietly walked close to the cattle. Then, still not uttering a sound, he advanced rapidly upon the cattle, unfolded the sheet quickly and shook it at them. Pandemonium! Even fairly gentle cattle can't stand much of that, especially in the middle of a dark, moonless night. Predictably, they stampeded away from the big white booger, and just got up good running speed when they came to this approximately 10-to-12 foot chainlink fence, but there was no stopping now! Their speed and weight—combined with their terror—took them through the fence, which almost disintegrated under the onslaught.

In two minutes the cattle were out of sight, and the fence was down for some 30 feet. The cowboy folded up the sheet, walked out the hole the cattle had made, and met the other rider who was leading his horse, mounted and rode off. In about an hour men and horses and cattle were peacefully grazing or sleeping.

Amazing sidenote: nothing more was ever said about the incident by Peter Pan or the ranch—it was as if the whole episode had never happened.

Fred Cable Sr., the man who had the Mobil gas station on the corner of Big Bear Boulevard and Pine Knot, is the hero of our next golfing episode, and no wonder; I have been told that he dearly loved the game of golf and played frequently and well. He was a genuine old-timer in Big Bear, the first of two or three generations who have lived here. If Fred Cable was the hero, and he was, then I was the villain, though luckily I kept him from probably a little or a lot of hurt.

This was in the 1950's when the Hamilton Brothers had bought out Jim Stocker, and they were now running the IS. I was alone, on horseback, and up on the ridge behind Moonridge looking for cattle that weren't supposed to be there, when I ran into a big white-faced cow with long horns and a big spring calf. I jumped her from above, without meaning to, but she, being a little bronco anyway, feeling good and heading downhill, really poured herself and her big calf off that mountainside. It was all I could do to keep up with the noise of the rolling rocks and the busting brush, but in about a mile she came out on relatively flat country at approximately the south end of Elm Street in Moonridge.

The cow and the calf were hot and runny by now and totally out of control, no stopping or turning them at this time, and they were separating, so I roped the calf and when he bawled, the old cow came back to fight. So I had some difficulty tying him down, but finally accomplished it. Then the old cow took off straight east toward the golf course and in due time got there, high headed, hot, mad and on the fight.

As she crossed Club View just south of Willow Avenue, she was headed for a green and a tee by some big old stand-out, stand-alone pines, and I was just about 50 yards behind her. She and I both looked up and guess who was about to tee off—yeah, Fred Cable Sr.

She must have looked about like a freight train bearing down upon him, because when she spotted him she made a beeline for him, blowing blood and snot out of her nose and beginning to run stiff-legged as cattle are prone to do when they are charging.

Well, for better or worse, Fred didn't look or act scared, and worse still he didn't bother getting behind one of those pine trees, but stood his ground. Although I was dumbfounded and very apprehensive about what might happen in the next 20 or so seconds, Fred just swung his golf club back up over his shoulder like it was a baseball bat and prepared to swing on that old high-horned cow when she got close enough.

Needless to say, I was much more scared than Cable, because I couldn't imagine that club doing any more damage than a flyswatter. I had already taken my rope down and built a loop as we came through the brush, because it was obvious she was only going to be stopped at the end of a rope. This development only sharply reduced the time I had and that old horse (Chub) was shoveling on the coal and we were rapidly overtaking her.

But it looked to me like it was at best going to be a dead heat. She would get to Fred just about the same time I got to her. Besides I might miss with the rope, as I frequently do. Meanwhile Fred was now all drawn back like he was going to knock a homer, and I was dying inside. Fred really didn't have a ghost of a chance of not being hurt, or something a lot worse. He weighed 180, she 1100. He was standing still, and she was going like the milltails of Hell.

Well, to make a drawn out story shorter, sharp spurs, a good running horse, a lucky catch and I brought that cow to a stop—after throwing, catching her horns, dallying and stopping my running horse —within three feet of Fred Cable. Both the cow and Chub slipped and skidded for 50 feet when Chub set up to stop her; both almost went down. And do you know, Fred never did look or act scared, nor say he was, and as for me—I never told him my heart was in my mouth and I was really terrified of what I thought was about to happen.

I let that old cow lead me over near the road where I spilled her and tied her down, and Fred by then was 200 yards down the fairway nonchalantly continuing his golf game, not realizing he had just experienced a happening as symbolic as a hole-in-one, and equally as lucky.

By evening we had brought the ranch truck to Moonridge and loaded the cow and calf into it. We hauled them to Baldwin Lake and released them into a bunch of gentle cattle. That old cow was still unhappy with the world and none, beast or human, felt up to challenging her.

Shay's Meadow at Baldwin Lake in the 1930's, with the Talmadge herd readying for the Fall drive to the desert. Will Talmadge—on 'Buddy'—is in the foreground.

Chapter Thirteen

ᏨᏲᎤ

Shay Ranch Cowboys

The Shay and Barker Ranch, using the club brand and the CO brand, was in operation before the turn of the century. Their summer range was what is now Baldwin Lake and Big Bear City, and they also ran at Dead Man's Lake (now Lake Williams) and the El Pinon Ranch (now Camp Oaks). Green Canyon and Red Canyon were also part of their range.

Uncle Will Shay married my grandmother's sister, Sarah, and had three sons and a daughter. The sons rode and worked on the ranch for many years.

The beef-fattening field was Shay Meadow, a fine mountain meadow now covered with fences, houses, paved roads and other pretty signs of progress. The beautiful ponds and smalls lakes and year-round streams are much changed from that yesteryear setting. "What year-round stream?" you may well ask—it is gone now!

The winter range for the Shay cattle was Coyote (between Joshua Tree and Twentynine Palms and now called Sunfair), Surprise Springs, and what is now Joshua Tree National Monument. At that time we called it the Quail, the Queen, Stubby, the Horse, et cetera, after the waterhole or spring in each area. It also included Barker tanks and Smith Canyon and Smith Canyon windmill.

The Shay Ranch hands included Uncle Will and his three sons Wynn, Cliff, and Brud, as well as Homer Urton and Jim Dever. They were rough-country, mountain-desert cowboys, and they had reason to be wild and woolly because the Shay cattle were known to be wild and woolly, hard to gather and spooky to handle.

Uncle Jack Dunlap, from the Yucaipa Ranch, married my grandmother's older sister, Elizabeth, and frequently rode on the Talmadge and Shay Ranches. He always maintained that the Shay cattle were wild in a peculiar way, inasmuch as "you couldn't catch them with a race horse in the morning, but could pat them on the ass by evening."

The Shay Ranch had many good horses down through the years. Three of the best were 'Sheep', 'Flag' and a big black and white Appaloosa whose name I cannot recall. Good horses, good hands and three wild, rough riding sons is what made that ranch "go round" successfully. Will Shay was of the stuff the "Old West" was made of; a book could be written about his life—but, it would be pretty salty!

Chapter Fourteen

∾

Old Bill Was Out of Tobacco

This story kind of wanders around all over the San Bernardinos from Big Bear to the Pipes Ranch to Rattlesnake Canyon. It's just a yarn, but interesting and true.

Seems sometime back in the late '30's old man Jacobi's grocery store in Big Bear City caught fire and it looked like, for a while, it was going to be a total. Now it was only a joke, but about that time the rumor was going around that Bear Valley Fire Department had saved more lots and fireplaces than any fire department in California.

Anyway, myself, Bill Betterley and Bill Shay were driving by and saw the predicament and stopped to help, and all three worked like dogs for over an hour hauling cases of canned vegetables and fruit, as well as every other imaginable thing in a grocery store. We had almost emptied the store out when they finally got everything under control —extensive damage but far from totaled.

When it was all over, the three of us—hot, begrimed and pooped— decided to take a carton of cigarettes and hide them in the weeds and sagebrush across the street, which we did. Jacobi had already said 'thanks'. But we found, when we went back after them the next day, that we hadn't put anything over on him, because he had gone across the street, taken the carton of Lucky Strikes and left us a carton of Wings. Even though we felt kind of sheepish over the theft, we laughed our heads off over the subtle little game he was playing with us.

About two days later both Bills, myself and Uncle Will Talmadge left by horseback for the Pipes Ranch to check on the ranch, the alfalfa, the fruit trees and the extensive vegetable garden. We also were to check on the water intake up the Pipes Canyon and gather any strays in the area, drive them back to the high meadows, and get all the calves branded.

Uncle Will was very tolerant and allowed us to play and race and have fun, even though he well knew the old adage that "one boy is one boy, two boys are half a boy and three boys are no boy at all." But he figured he could get all the work and gathering and driving done by hollering at us once in a while, so he had allowed us all to go.

As usual when going down Rattlesnake to Antelope—and not pushed for time—we stopped at Bill Kramer's cabin in Sleepy Hollow. He always had a drink of cool water and some cookies that he would bring up on his homemade dumbwaiter from the cellar; a spring ran there the year around and it was almost as good as an icebox. He frequently saw no one for a month at a time, and the road ended at his house—you could not drive to Rose Mine. He and his dog "Policeman" were always eager to visit, but this time he was particularly unhappy. He had run out of tobacco about three weeks before, and was smoking a mixture of coffee, willow leaves and bark!

So the three of us got our heads together and, unknown to Uncle Will (he would have kicked our butts if he had known about the cigarettes), got old Bill Kramer off to the side. We gave him some cigarettes and swore him to secrecy. Needless to say he was the happiest man from Baldwin Lake to the Pipes (the only one, too) and we felt we had really done our good deed.

At that point he couldn't wait for us to get out of there so he could have a smoke.

We went on to the Pipes, did the necessary checking and gathering, and about two days later were going back up Rattlesnake with ten head of strays and three or four little calves. Because they were all gentle and those old native cows knew the trail to Big Bear as well as we did and wanted to get there once they were started, we felt safe in going up Sleepy Hollow Canyon to Bill Kramer's for more cookies and conversation.

When we were at the Pipes, the three of us yonkers got to feeling badly, because we didn't normally smoke, didn't know how to smoke and didn't even like to smoke. We had decided unanimously not to waste any more cigarettes on ourselves, but save them all for old Bill when we went back past his canyon on our way to Rose Mine.

So this time when we went in for cookies, he took us aside and said he was out of cigarettes again. I can truthfully say we made him the happiest man in the San Bernardinos when we each gave him a couple of packs of Wings. Even though that brand was pretty much an inferior blend, they looked good to him and he fell forever in our debt.

Bill Kramer was a nice guy, and completely dependent on friends for groceries, cigarettes and everything else; he didn't have a car, and though people brought him things, seems sometimes they forgot him. He was a World War I Veteran who had been heavily gassed with Mustard Gas when he was with the famous American "Lost Batallion" on the front in France. Only a small group survived that ordeal, and he suffered several bullet and shrapnel wounds as well as the gassing. He sometimes never left Sleepy Hollow from one year's end to the next. Doctors had recommended the high, dry air for his lungs (probably 5,000 feet). Course I guess he shouldn't have been smoking, but three boys were not inclined nor even about to lecture a war hero.

All three of us to this day remember Bill, his dog "Policeman", his dumbwaiter, his swinging dog door so Policeman could go in and out; also his homemade cookies—they were really good. His spring-house-cellar combination was also unique and successful. For an old batch, he had fixed things up very nice for himself, especially considering that his Army pension and his own ingenuity were his only assets.

Chapter Fifteen

ᏄᎳᏅ

World's Championship Endurance Horse Race

John Talmadge, my grandfather, was a good friend, contemporary and school chum of Card Pew. Card's claim to fame most of his life was his ability to tip himself up on his hands and walk for several steps or 100 yards, going up and down curbs with ease—where they existed in the 1870's and 1880's—showing no special effort or stress. It really had no particular importance at the time but can you imagine what that was doing to his arm, shoulder and chest muscles? Obvious, eh?

Several years later there came to San Bernardino the world's champion endurance rider. The name is long forgotten, but he was from one of the New England states originally and, according to handed down data, had won his championship in one of the Southwestern states.

A match race for the title was arranged and Card Pew was chosen to ride against this World's Champion. The distance would be 50 miles, and the course a one-mile circular track near Hot Creek (East Baseline). Each rider would choose the best 10 horses he could find, and have a crew of four to saddle, lead, hold, start and control the nine horses not in use. The spectators included somewhere near 50% of San Bernardino's population, plus some from L.A., Riverside, Colton and other areas.

Both had 10 good horses, the judges and timekeepers were carefully chosen and on the given time, on the given hour and at the given minute the race began.

By the time two horses were exchanged (one change each mile), the strength that Card Pew had in his entire upper torso and arms had already allowed him to open a significant lead, which he maintained and lengthened as the race progressed. His physical prowess allowed him to dismount and run to the next horse and then, due to this great strength, the horse holders could start the horse as soon as Card had one hand on the horn of the saddle. He was able in every instance to

66

complete his mount while the horse was accelerating to a full run, and consequently and subsequently he won the endurance race hands down. He won by over a quarter of a mile, and led from mile one to mile 50.

Card went to the dance that night; however, the then ex-world champion was completely tuckered out and was taken to his room, attended by a doctor, and put to bed.

This is one of several of the types of races that the old-timers used to enjoy and bet on. They also enjoyed a matched race between two horses whose owners were willing to bet the farm, and sometimes did. A common bet was horse against horse—winner take all—but that type of race almost does not exist at this time.

Cattle ranch scene at Big Bear Lake over 60 years ago.

∽

Chapter Sixteen

Cowboys & Horses: Hard Riding Teams

The Swarthout and Gentry (Heart Bar) Ranch summered its cattle in Big Meadows, Cienega Seco, Fish Creek, Broom Flats and Santa Ana Canyon, including Seven Oaks and almost to Mentone. "Swarty," as he was called, was the working partner. He ran the ranch and lived at Big Meadows in the summertime and Old Woman Springs in the winter. His partner, Dale Gentry, owned the California Hotel and Ford agency in San Bernardino and lived there the year-round.

Swarty, a small man physically, ran the toughest ranch of the four and made up for his small size by having and using what was obviously a high IQ. For instance, he could not use a wagon or truck on his drive, because of the country being so unfriendly, so he loaded three or four jackasses with bedrolls and beef and beans, and they followed the herd along from camp to camp. (Many of the feral burros in the Santa Ana Canyon and Seco areas are descendants of Swarty's pack burros.) He and Charlie Reche—the man who Willie Boy* shot—are credited with thinking up, figuring out, and digging the hole that resulted in syphoning 150 miner's inches of irrigation water at Old Woman Springs. A miner's inch is the amount of water which comes through a one-inch pipe one foot high, and hits ground one foot in front of the pipe. Prior to this, there had been only a small spring on the fault that can be traced from Twentynine Palms to Grapevine Canyon.

The Heart Bar cattle were known to be wild and skittish and very apt to run when you jumped them, but Swarty had such cowboys as Charlie Reche, Clay Lewis and Howard Whipple. These were all

---

*Willie Boy gained national attention in the fall of 1909 when he killed Chemehuevi Indian Mike Boniface near Banning and kidnapped his daughter whom he wished to be his bride. What would have been regarded as simply another unimportant Indian quarrel, by a stroke of fate, mushroomed to epic proportions and resulted in a long, arduous manhunt involving county officials and a large posse.

tough, rough-country, wild-cattle, hot desert and cold mountain cowboys, at home and competent with such country and such cattle.

The winter range of the Heart Bar was headquartered at Old Woman Springs, and ran from Mound Springs to Lucerne Valley and from Rock Corral to Duncan Flat; also on the low desert from Old Woman to Mesquite Springs and Means Dry Lake, including what has, in recent years, become notorious as a fly-in field for dope of all kinds—Soggy Dry Lake.

Swarty also released several good cold-blooded mares in his back country and then put a good American saddle-bred stud to run with them. He thus bred and raised some of the best, surefooted, rough country-wise, mountain-bred, desert-smart horses ever seen in the San Bernardino Mountains. I have since learned that the American saddle-bred horse has a good or better bone than any other breed of horse, with the possible exception of the Arabian, and that only when the Arabian is in North Africa or the Near East. The Arabian, when raised there, is reputed to have the hardest bone of any mammal on this earth, but when imported elsewhere, the hardness diminishes. It has something to do with the dry, strong native feed in the Arab countries, the Sinai and Sahara deserts.

So again the experience and expertise of the old cattlemen becomes evident. The more you study them, their work, their methods, their improvisations, the smarter and more interesting they appear.

As an example of the athletic ability of the Heart Bar horses, I remember one time when we were camped at Round Valley for a few days, where both the IS and the Heart Bar were represented. We were there for the express purpose of getting a small bunch of wild cattle out of Upper Antelope and that general area. The cattle we were after had been seen in that area by both ranches, and consisted of some old wild cows with calves and several older orahanas (unmarked and unbranded cattle). They were just as wild as the deer that they practically ran with, and we ended up getting about six head out in about five days.

This one day I was riding with Heart Bar cowboy Howard Whipple, IS cowboy Bud Waite and John Talmadge, when we jumped a big cow with a four-month-old calf. My granddad, John Talmadge, roped the cow in the first half mile. He was riding a big buckskin, half-thoroughbred he called Golden Ace, and riding that good, fast horse got him to the cow first.

He and Bud Waite were handling the cow all right, so Howard

and I turned down a little canyon full of rocks, brush, oaks and pinon, where we had seen the calf disappear. In a couple hundred yards we jumped the calf again and that little white-face—as only long-legged, scared, wild calves can do—took off at about 100 m.p.h. right down the steep side hill. In about another 300 yards Howard caught up to the calf on one of those good, young, well-broke Swarthout home-grown horses and roped him, jumped off, and wrestled and tied the little bull calf down.

My horse had gone down in a big pile of downed scrub oak limbs, and by the time I brushed off, checked the horse for wear and tear from the fall and caught up to him, Howard had just tied the calf down. But the annoying thing was, his horse had caught the calf and come to a stop in a pile of boulders on the steep side hill, and it took him ten minutes to lead that horse out of the spot where he had run, full tilt, and caught up to a calf that was panic stricken and flying.

That is as good an example as I can think of to show the things that a good mountain cow horse had to do to get his end of the work successfully completed. The rocky, steep area where that horse came to a stop was impossible for a horse to walk over—only his speed and momentum and athletic ability got him out into the middle of that rock pile. He didn't fall going in or coming out, but he entered in about five seconds or less and, as I said, he scrambled, scratched and balanced on the rocks, slipped and all but fell several times in the 10 minutes it took him to get out of that particular spot.

Amazing? Yes. Unusual? A little. Part of the horse's job? Yes. Part of the cowboy's job? Darn right. Dangerous? You bet! Howard Whipple was some kind of a brave hombre matched up with a brave equine athlete, both matched against a wild, four-legged flying machine, who was running in total panic.

Chapter Seventeen

⁓

The Wild Bull and the One-Lunger

Bob Hitchcock is the best football coach by far that Temple City ever had, and I really think if he had just stayed with it he could also have become a fair-to-middlin' cowpuncher. At any rate, and good help is admittedly hard to find, he and I were gathering some remnant cattle belonging to Hamilton Ranch, trying to gather them all as the ranch was going out of business; we were camped at and working out of Coxey Ranch.

We had discovered tracks and seen glimpses of a few head of "wild" or "orahana" cattle, but up to this time always had our hands full of semi-gentle cattle. Being unable to give our full attention to the outlaw types, we had up to now ignored them.

But on this particular day, coming up Coxey Creek about a half-mile below the Ranch, a big red several-years-old orahana bull, seeing the cattle but not spotting us, came trotting out of the heavy pinon and chaparral growth. He bawled and approached the gentle cattle, his whole attention being held by the cows in the bunch which he was soon checking out. Invariably, as he worked his way down through the 20 or so head we had, he finally spotted us, at which point his whole attitude changed. He broke up the hill with me pursuing on a big rough brown ranch horse (can't remember his name) and in about 600 yards the area, while still heavy with pinon, became more open and somewhat level. This honest, trying old horse put me up there and I roped him and brought him to a stop, but that wasn't the end of this incident. It turned out to be a blessing that the pinons were fairly thick, because that bull turned and came back down the rope almost immediately. Dodging him became a full-time occupation as he would charge, try to run off and then—when stopped—immediately charge again. By hook or by crook, and after choking him down pretty well, I managed to tie him to a pinon. I was removing my saddle to cool out the horse's back and let him get his air when Bob caught up with me,

71

having put the cattle we had inside the lower Coxey gate before tracking me down.

The bull, too smart to choke himself down, was also getting his second wind. When I re-saddled, Bob decided to have me turn the bull loose after we heeled him and put his rope on the bull's horns. Bob was going to lead, drive, follow, drag or tease him toward the Coxey fenced field. The only problem was, he was riding a tall, slim, part thoroughbred colt; he was young and only partly broke, the type the Hitchcocks called a "One lunger", and the name was not a compliment. Most such built horses do not, in the long run, make it on a cow ranch, and typically this one did not (I think his real name was Red Racer). By the next year he was gone, but this summer Bob was stuck with him, and now leading out a big orahana bull on him was a recipe for disaster.

We got along fairly well for the mile or so back to Coxey, the bull leading us part of the way, and being led by Bob and "hurrahed" by me the other. Then, when we had it made, were inside the fence and all seemed in good order, the bull charged the Red Racer and hit him from behind, almost knocking him down and scaring him so bad that the colt broke in two. After a few good jumps he bucked Bob off right in front of the charging bull, and for a few seconds it was nip and tuck and fraught with danger.

These happenings teeter on very dangerous ground, but on the other side of the coin they are over for better or worse almost instantly. I did the best I could to get the attention of the bull away from Bob, but in truth he turned and ran back toward the bush on his own, and although a-foot, Bob was okay. By this time of course it became very funny to have seen Bob bucked off and trying to dodge the bull, and I could hardly ride over and retrieve his horse, but I did. I believe if he hadn't been so eager to get back on and go after the bull he would have cleaned my plow, and I would have been totally helpless with laughter. As we were pursuing the bull seconds later and I was still almost rolling off the horse with mirth, he growled, "That wasn't all that ——— funny."

Anyway, we caught up with the bull, picked up the rope and got him into the corral, and during all of it bad names were unmercifully hurled at me, and even mean statements made about my ancestors. However, while we were cooking dinner that night on the big old wood cook stove at Coxey, Bob finally saw the humor in the situation and got off my case, and eventually laughed as hard as I. I didn't really blame him, because as they say about flying, it is hours of tedium and boredom, interspersed with moments of sheer terror.

Of course, part of his ill temper was caused by my reminder that just about a hundred yards from there, during the summer before, a good little sorrel horse he owned had bucked him off one early crisp morning, and I had laughed my head off then too—as soon as I had determined that he wasn't dead. Very thin-skinned, that Hitchcock.

Chapter Eighteen

ༀ

Roping Wild Bulls

One day a few years ago, three of us—Frank, Rolly, and myself—were in Coyote Canyon in San Diego County, hunting for wild orahana cattle, and had the good fortune to jump three orahana bulls. Running up over a ridge just ahead of us were one large bull with bad horns, one medium bull probably three or four years old, and the third a smaller two-year-old. Did they hear us or smell us? *Quien sabes?* Anyway, it made little difference, for they weren't sticking around.

It was rough cholla-and-chaparral country, but in a short ways we were pushing them. The medium-sized brockled-faced bull broke off to himself and Frank and Rolly took after him. I followed the other two and in about a mile they broke off into an open and smoother area and I was able to overtake and rope the smaller two-year-old.

Encountering no big trouble, but in a hurry, I tied him to a Joshua tree with my lass rope. I could do this because I caught him by the horns and he couldn't fight it and choke himself to death. But he could run to the end of the rope and spill himself, which he promptly did. But everything, tree, rope and his neck, held, and I took off hurriedly on the track of the big bull. I tracked him about two miles at a trot until, from on top of a little ridge, I could see him, slowed to a walk about 300 yards ahead of me in fairly flat but bushy country which was continuously cut by little washes, and occasional stands of big wash willows.

Keeping the bull in sight, I slowed to a walk long enough to let my horse (Bad Eye) catch his air and cool out a little. Then I overtook and jumped the bull, who by this time was tired, hot, mad and full of fight.

Then I ran him. He could run a little, surprisingly, for so big a bull, for about a half-mile trying to get close enough to rope him. But each time I pushed too close he would (all 1,500 pounds of him with those foot-long horns) stop, turn and pursue me and old Bad-Eye for 50 to 100 yards, then veer off and continue running. Finally, I tried to stop—or at least deter—him by shooting my .38 special right down over the rear of the horse and just in front of the bull's nose as he was charging. This was no mean trick, while in the rough, going and running, and being as careful as possible so the horse would not fall while being that closely pursued. Anyway, even in two or three attempts, the shots right in his face proved completely ineffectual and deterred him not at all.

Eventually he stopped to fight, breathing heavily, shaking his horns and blowing snot all over. Coward that I am, I kept to the opposite side of a very large, rank cholla and let my horse, who was showing wear and tear, breathing hard and trembling with fatigue, get himself together. We took 15 minutes for everyone to recoup. By good luck, I got the bull to come around the cholla to fight and got both his front feet in my loop. By a big effort on Bad Eyes' part, we pulled him—mad and fighting—right down into the cholla, which didn't do a thing to gentle his spirit. How happy would you be with a big cholla on the end of your nose?

While I could hold him down, I couldn't readily go any farther with him. Besides, I was sure the others would, eventually, track me down and help me out of this situation. Having lost the bull they went after, they showed up in about 20 or 30 minutes—much to my delight. Not quite like having a bear by the tail, but it approximated such a predicament. With their assistance, the bull was soon securely tied down and I could take the saddle off Bad Eye and air and cool his back. He had been as hot as a $2 pistol on at least three occasions during that chase, and heaved a sigh of delight when the cool air hit him.

We all then returned to where the pickup trucks were parked, and got a drink and a bite to eat. Then we drove over to where I tied the little bull, loaded him without untoward incident and tied him to the foot of the rack by a cow halter.

The two of them, Frank and Rolly, got to laughing and I curiously asked, "*Que paso?*" They admitted that as they came to the little bull while tracking me down, one of them spotted the critter and said, "There's one," and the bull was standing there looking at them. They took down their ropes and built to him. This, of course, startled him, and he broke and ran some distance away, with them in hot pursuit. About that time he came to the end of my first lass rope and did a complete "Hoolahan," ending up flat on his back, and they—then realizing he was already tied—had a good laugh about their little ploy.

We then went back to where the big bull with the bad horns was tied down, and positioned the trucks to get ready to load him. When he saw us, he struggled mightily and succeeded in getting halfway up, and then fell back. We, at the time, did not realize it, but he had strained and stretched the rope tying his legs until he had a certain amount of slack.

We got the truck up close in order to load him and went in close, on horseback, to put ropes on his head to lead him with, or drag him. At this time he was red-eyed: glistening, irredescent red-eyed, an animal "berserk" if there ever was one. At any rate, and almost tragically, I made the mistake of getting between him and the truck, and he chose that moment, because of our proximity, to make the supreme effort to get to his feet, taking full advantage of the slack that his prior struggles had caused. He was able to get to his feet and charge me, even though his front feet were still tied together.

With amazing speed and evil, mad aforethought, he pinned Bad Eye and me against the side of the three-quarter-ton Chevy four-wheel-drive pickup. He then pushed against the horse so hard that my leg on the other side of the horse, driven against the side of the bed of the pickup, pushed the metal in two to three inches for a length of two feet. Then he hooked again and this time found Bad Eye's right rump to the tune of 55 stitches.

Then the phenomenon occurred for which there seems no logical explanation, but it happened: the bull—with his powerful neck muscles —lifted the horse suddenly into the air, and the sudden violent movement propelled me over the saddle horn, without touching it. I found myself astride the horse's neck, but only momentarily, because within a split second the bull shifted to the forward part of Bad Eye, hooked viciously upward again and I, totally involuntarily—was propelled up and back over the horn, again without touching it, into the seat of the saddle where the episode had begun. At that moment, about 30 seconds after the melee started, the bull, who had been floundering and fighting for his footing all the while, tripped over the ropes that were half holding him and went down, and I finally spurred Bad Eye out of harms way.

By that time the blood was running down his hind leg and pooling on the ground and I knew he would have to visit a vet as soon as possible. (This was 3:30 p.m., and it was midnight in Cherry Valley before I found a vet on duty on Sunday). But, of course, the bleeding had coagulated and while he was stiff and sore, definitely was not about to bleed to death. Bad Eye never faltered, though it must have smarted just a little. We got the ropes on and dragged the bull onto the truck and tied him in and headed out for Anza—over 15 miles of really bad road.

Then it was on to the butcher. We couldn't lay over anywhere because they, the truly wild orahana cattle, will not eat or drink when first penned up, but just walk the corral fence and pursue anything that moves and some things that don't. They lose 150 pounds in the chase, tying down, loading and hauling. The sooner you can get them butchered the better, because the weight loss continues and intensifies when they refuse to eat or drink for the first few days of captivity. Besides, they are downright dangerous, to people, other animals and even other cattle.

We were removing these bulls from a state park because they wanted the feed and freedom and outback country for mountain sheep and other authentic wild animals and varmits that we all like to see, photograph, and study; and this in their natural habitat.

Chapter Nineteen

ᘓ

High Chaparral

High Chaparral. That is probably one of the most romantic of all descriptions of a Western cattle ranch. Why?

Well, when it is no longer high chaparral on a cattle range it becomes a cleared off, bulldozed, leveled off, promotional scheme of some promoter who will sell off lots and houses and stores and shopping areas for a big development. They still insist on calling it progress. But that is depressing—let's get on with it and talk and write about that which still remains, while there is still something left to exclaim over.

High Chaparral was even the name of one of my favorite television series, one I wish was still on; never missed it! What is chaparral? It's a group or series of short, hard-leaved growths, both tree and shrub. Over a hundred such type plants grow in Southern California. The word comes from "chaparro" which means "live oak" in Spanish—and that is one type of tree that makes up this unusual mixed growth.

The main plants making up the most of "high chaparral" are red shank, manzanita, chemise, scrub oak, sagebrush, sumac and buckthorn. These are mixed with many others depending on various factors.

It was once a source of food, and manzanita berries, acorns and several other plants, roots, seeds, flowers and leaves were used by Indians. Many were even used by the early Spanish, Mexican and Anglo pioneers.

During the days of campfires, outdoor water heating, wood burning stoves and fireplaces, it was an excellent source of such fuel and still is in many areas. And much of it and its roots are excellent hardwood fuel, better than many other wood fuels such as pine.

The wood is also an excellent source of fencing material, particularly for the fence posts themselves, but also could be and was used for the entire fence when necessary in the absence of metal wire.

Its present value in the main is claimed to be its ground water conservation process through the root systems to protect valuable watersheds. It also can be noted, however, that it is not a 100 percent blessing, because each such tree or brush in most cases also drinks hundreds of gallons of water, particularly during the dry season. If water is not available for its needs, it becomes a critical fire hazard, and when set becomes an all but unmanageable fire. Its blessings are mixed at best.

High chaparral is especially noted because it is a wide swath of living beautiful flora that grows so well and successfully in areas where rainfall is sparse. It grows where most of the plants of the earth do not and cannot thrive and where the soil itself is frequently arid, dry, rocky and uncomforting to any growth. But miraculously the members of the high chaparral family grow, flourish, bloom and spread their abundant seeds over the wide landscape, a truly remarkable achievement when you examine its environs. It needs to be a survivor and it needs to be tough, and it is both.

Without the chaparral growth the areas so covered would be desolate and barren indeed. The fauna would be practically non-existent and the millions of cattle and millions of pounds of beef so fed and grown in the last centuries would have been impossible. It boils down to the fact that the world would indeed be poorer but for the areas of the high chaparral and what it protects and produces from so little.

Cattle ranching and cowpunching becomes an art of its own in such country with such growth—hard to see in, hard to handle or find cattle in—and difficult for horses to negotiate through, particularly at a run. It does have the effect of making good cowboys and good horses; and those who have experienced it are better for it.

A roper in such country must run under very difficult circumstances and catch in one of the few small openings where he is able to swing his loop. Every 100 yards to one-half mile, such an opening exists. A roper must enter such small areas right on the critter's tail to be able to swing and catch before it enters the brush again that is just a few feet in front of it. Like I said, good cowboys and good horses—no relationship to arena roping.

No offense though. Calf roping and team roping as well as steer jerking, team tying and ribbon jerking are all great sport, fun, interesting and habit forming just like a drug, but there is no comparing the two—as they do in so many advertisements these days. One is the "real thing;" the other is facsimile at best.

The real thing is done without music, band, flags, spectators, judges, stop watches and time penalties. You're on your own and your horse can fall, a limb could knock you off your horse, a mean critter could hook your horse badly, or whatever else may, could and does happen. There is no doctor or ambulance or paramedics within miles and probably no road either.

Dangerous? That's the reason it's done, talked about, relived and storied. It is a small, holy grail to a cowboy like a kachina is to an Indian and held as the most special, inspirational and sought-after activity in every "hand's" life. (Right after girls, of course. You really can't figure girls into the quotation fairly, since we all freely admit their special status.)

You like cowboys being given the royal, green light treatment? You can probably expect more, but as Madden said, "Don't pay attention to the blind horse, just load the wagon."

Cattle graze at Coxey Meadow on a drive from the Los Flores Ranch to Big Bear. Coxey Meadow was at one time the site of a U.S. Ranger Station.

Chapter Twenty

∽

Locoweed & Sand

SCARLETT LOCOWEED — *Astragalus Coccineus,* of the Pea family; the bright scarlett flowers make it one of the most vividly colorful plants of the desert. Common on the Mojave Desert, its leaf and root are very similar to Death Valley Locoweed. Its effect is at least similar. DESERT RATTLEWEED — *Astragalus Crotalariae Davidsoni,* also of the Pea family. Reddish purple flower, mostly found on the Mojave Desert. Similar leaf, root, color and evil appearance. MOJAVE LOCOWEED — *Astragalus Mohavensis* of the Pea family, too, as are all local locoweed species. Has a rose-purple flower. Grows on the high and dry slopes of the Mojave Desert as well as in the Mojave North and East valleys. Also similar coloring, root system, leaf and luciferic appearance if you stare at it long enough.

All types produce, later in the year, the hollow, bulbous, rattles that pop when stepped on—and that is an indication that it is locoweed of one type or another.

So, what are we saying? Well, simply that there are at least three species on the Mojave, all very similar and, without their blooms, difficult to tell one from the other. And they almost give a warning by their appearance, and of course, their very presence is a warning to range cattle, sheep and horse owners to beware, and to watch for its evil side and its noticable harmful effects.

They say it takes about 60 pounds of it to ruin a horse, and a certain amount (unknown to me) to affect cattle. However, during the Spring when there is lots of green feed, cattle and horses ignore it or only take a mouthful occasionally, along with many mouthfuls of flowers, filaree, bunch grass, etc., and thus it does no harm. Those small amounts to all appearances apparently have no effect, or at least no noticeable bad effect.

Just what does it do? It was given its present name by the early Spaniards, and as is commonly known, the Spanish word "Loco" means "crazy". That quite well pictures what happens to sheep, cattle and horses, and eventually they will die of its consumption. The author has seen semi-wild feral horses in the Mojave Desert that were affected, and it is apparent that the insidious properties in Locoweed can cause an irreversable injury to the brain of horses, cattle and sheep.

There are two general types in the U.S. Southwest, the *Astragalus* and *Oxytropis*. The various species of the Mojave Desert appear all to be of the *Astragalus* type.

How does it show up on the animals? Just like so called crazy people, each individual may react somewhat differently. The animals trot with a very high, elongated, exaggerated step with their front feet, and appear to not see well, fall over bushes and rocks that ordinary critters would readily avoid. Some have a blank and stupid look in their faces and eyes, unseeing, unthinking, unable to cope. They grow thinner and thinner, and have been known to come in to a waterhole after not having drank for two or more days, stop some 20 feet short of the spring, waterhole, or trough, and noisily suck air for several minutes. They then would turn and walk unsteadily back into the dry desert or foothill area and not come back for a day or so. Upon returning they would be thinner, more loco, thirstier, and on this trip might actually drink. At this junction it was of course necessary to destroy the animal, actually putting them out of their misery.

When does this usually occur and why? Locoweed has a long tap root, and in Summer and Fall when almost all the grasses and flowers on the desert have dried up, the long tap root is still finding deep moisture for the locoweed, similar to an alfalfa tap root. At this point, the locoweed stays green and becomes more attractive to livestock and at this time their choice — if in large amounts — may very well live up to its name. Cattle, horse and sheep men dread these times, and attempt to move the stock to areas where the weed is less prevelant. Also, stockmen have rooted it out, poisoned it, fought it, but it is a long way from the endangered species list and everyone expects it to be with us for a long time to come. Some phoney, nuevo-pseudo environmentalists will probably prefer it to sheep, cattle and horses, and attempt to have a National Monument set aside for all species of locoweed. If he or they do, we will all suspect they have been eating too much of it.

A similar appearing situation, mostly in horses, can occur when the horse remuda is turned out on dry pasture or hillside areas in the late Fall, particularly after a Fall rain has flattened the filaree down against sandy soil. This is the start of a chain of events that find the horses, who prefer filaree, green or dry, to almost anything else, trying and succeeding in picking up the flattened runners of the filaree with their lips; the evil in this is that with each bite so obtained, the horse also picks up a few grains of sand, which under ordinary conditions and in small amounts can be readily passed by the horse. But when that is the preponderant feed for the horse over several weeks, the sand does not pass through, and if you put your ear on a stethoscope next to his belly, you can hear the sand grinding around in there. If nothing is done at this point, or it begins to accumulate in a large ball in the horse's belly, his symptoms will be very similar to a loco horse. The author, who is not a veterinarian, cannot readily tell the difference between loco and sanded from simple observation, but both can be fatal or mentally crippling, to one degree or another. An old cow-horse named Jim McGinnis, on the Los Flores, was a good using horse until the loco hit him and then he would throw a complete fit. It happened almost once a day. Upon performing an objective autopsy on a horse that has died of or been put down because of sanding, a large ball of sand almost the size of a volley ball will be found, and in the ball will be found large brownish, white grubs the size of your thumb. That almost solid ball of sand cannot at that point be readily removed by any method but surgery, but earlier on a good physic given daily will remove the sand.

Sand or weed, they are just as mentally disturbed. If you suddenly appear, startle the horse and clap your hands and yell, either type of loco horse is very likely to rear up and fall over backward, get up with difficulty, wild eyed, trembling and almost fall while staggering off in the opposite direction. That actually was a rule of thumb test for loco, and the degree of reaction you got would be used to estimate the degree the animal was suffering from loco or sanding.

If caught soon enough, and the first mild reactions to locoweed or sanding are seen early on, it can be frequently cured completely by putting the affected horses on a pasture of green, damp, fresh alfalfa. This, of course, physics them almost violently and, (as Uncle Will described it), "they can thread a needle at thirty paces." But this only is effective if caught in the early stages, i.e., before the theoretical 60 pounds of loco have been eaten in a fairly short time, or before the sand has begun to harden into a ball in their bellies.

Locoweed is located in almost all parts of California, there being at least 62 varieties statewide. The plants are roughly similar in appearance and color, most all develop the "rattles" or "balloons" and all are poisonous to livestock in one form or another.

The poison involved had been recognized as being alkaloids; however, later work has left the identity of the toxic compond in doubt. But the serious loss of life in livestock makes further investigation and work desirable.

Cattle and sheep show symptoms in six to eight weeks and in an additional four to six weeks will die if the diet is not changed. Horses are much more susceptible, and the time between symptoms and death is much shorter. In horses, final stages are the inability to eat or drink, and paralysis. Horses in any observable stages of loco are dangerous to ride or drive, or even handle.

All animals find locoweeds distasteful at first, but if forced to eat them due to hunger, get hooked on them and often prefer it to anything else. If the diet is changed, an eventual recovery may be expected if the symptoms have not progressed too far.

In all cases, from all loco species, the symptoms are more violent and pronounced in horses, and death occurs in a shorter period. But with all victims, horses as well, the incidence of death may very well be spotty within an affected group of animals. Although the work done is not conclusive, it appears certain *Astragalus* species are more toxic than others; however, until more specific research is concluded, it is best to view all loco and rattleweed with suspicion.

Locoweed—as much a part of the West as Kit Carson—is just one more of the difficulties faced by owners of goats, sheep, cattle, and horses in the taming of the West. And it still exists, oft in profusion, on open rangeland whether private, railroad, school, B.L.M. or Forest Service. Admittedly, it is kind of romantic; who hasn't heard of locoweed in Western books, pictures, and T.V. serials? It is a great part of our heritage and lore, taking its place with wolves, grizzly bear, Johnny Appleseed, California's gold rush, the Donner Party, poisoned waterholes, the Alamo, barrel cactus and the Pony Express. It is one of the bad guys that became famous or notorious, such as Billy the Kid, John Wesley Hardin, Joaquin Murietta, Montana blizzards, Death Valley's heat, avalanches and deadly nightshade.

And we can hardly hold cattle and horses to blame if they, as was shown previously, get hooked on loco. Just look around at your relatives, neighbors, friends and acquaintances of the species *Homosapien* who are hooked on alcohol, marijuana, cocaine, heroin, crack, and hashish. Really, and as a matter of fact, look around you and see how smart cattle and horses suddenly become. Guess we shouldn't belabor this any further, though it is tempting, but probably more effective if each is allowed to ponder it in their own ways, and in their own time.

Rattleweed, Locoweed, *Astragalus, Oxytropis, Coccineus, Crotalariae;* even the sound of their names is ominous and somber, and to think that Sweet Peas and Snow Peas and canned baby Green Peas, which we have taken to our hearts, are first cousins of these terrors of the rangeland!

Edward West Case—father of Mary Rose Stone—near Palm Springs in 1925 with San Jacinto in background. Case was a horsetrader by profession and owner/operator of a livery stable in Palm Springs when that desert community was a sleepy village.

The author astride 'Golden Ace' while breaking him as a three-year-old at Yuma, Ariz., this in 1938. Ace was 1/2 thoroughbred and 1/2 work horse.

Mary Rose Stone (*nee* Case)
when she served as the
"Queen of the Rodeo". The a
proudly claims Mary his wife

This entourage of four bugg
and wagons (plus some 20 hc
is the Ed Case family as they
moved from Palm Springs to
Yuma in 1926.

ary Rose Stone in 1937 as Miss California and Miss Outdoor Girl in statewide competition at Salinas Rodeo.

Author on 'Rusty' during the 1970 Old Miners Days. Rusty was "a great littl horse who could do it all."

❦

Chapter Twenty-One

Ed Case: Shrewd Horseman

Old-time Big Bear Valley horse trader Edward West Case was the father of my wife, Mary Rose Louise. He was a shrewd horse trader and horse racer and not always entirely legal. Upon his death, his black leather box of medicines, potions, and syringes for horses was found to contain so many illegal, potent, touchy, poisonous, dangerous, narcotic substances that they promptly destroyed it. No one else knew how to properly use and administer them.

When he was 60 and 70 years old he was in frequent foot races for money against men 25 years or more his junior. He always ran with his high-heeled boots on, and almost always won. There was a monetary method in his madness. When he challenged some man several years younger than he to run 100-yards for $20, they could hardly refuse. He never raced for fun or to prove a point, only for money—be it a foot race or a horse race.

He was known as a harsh husband and father. For instance, when Mary Rose was 16 and won the Miss California contest in Salinas, Governor Merriam and others of note, plus everyone from the contest —several hundred people in all—were attending the big dance celebration, at which the guest of honor was to be the Mary Rose. Her father refused to let her attend—and she, the guest of honor, did not.

Dr. Von Gardner, a local San Bernardino oculist, however, who knew Ed Case well, stated—to my father-in-law's credit—that "Ed Case was the smartest man I ever knew." Present-day and old-time horse traders and horsemen with whom it has been the subject of conversation have, without exception, admitted that Ed Case was the best horseman, best non-licensed veterinarian and shrewdest horse trader they had ever known. Each had a yarn or two to spin to make their points valid. Happenings like the following crop up in the stories of Ed Case continually.

One day in the 1920's some 40 or 50 people were gathered to

watch a horse race between a half dozen of the fastest horses in the San Bernardino/Riverside/Ontario region, and each man had put up $10, thus making what in those days was a very respectable purse. Just about the time the race was getting ready to go, Ed Case came driving up in a buggy, pulled by an old, raw-boned, sway-backed horse in a blind bridle and accompanied by a young black boy. Ed yelled over at the starter, the judges, and the owners of the other horses and asked if anyone could get in the race. He was told it took just $10 to enter, which he promptly produced and said, "Wait a minute while I get my horse saddled." He walked over to where this old horse was standing with his head practically on the ground, to all appearances sound asleep, the trace chains still hooked and the shafts resting on the turf. He dug around in the back of the buggy and produced a racing saddle and bridle, took off the harness and hooked up the racing gear, then placed the black boy up on top of the horse.

The story is that the old horse straightened up, threw his head up in the air, got bug-eyed, tried to buck the boy off and snorted and pranced over to the starting line. Needless to say, the other owners and jockeys could already see the handwriting on the wall as it became apparent this old horse was an ex-racehorse, a thoroughbred off the big-time track. Ed had him so doped up, administered while saddling, that all the age, aches, pains and broken-down parts of that old horse weren't to be felt at all. He could have broken his leg and run on the stump for a half-mile without feeling it.

Naturally, he won the race and the money. An hour or two later the buzz wore off the old horse, and Ed and the boy harnessed him back up to the buggy and slowly rode into the sunset with the prize money. There was some ominous muttering, which Ed both enjoyed and ignored.

He was a cantankerous old character, but no one ever called him a stupid cantankerous old character, either to his face or behind his back. Half Indian and half French, it was an explosive mixture.

Chapter Twenty-Two

ოჯ

Tale of Early Rodeos

In the late 1940's Big Bear Lake had a brand-new riding, roping and rodeo club—the Vaqueros de las Montanas, "the Riders of the Mountains."

Two of the first projects decided upon were building a rodeo arena and buying roping calves for all members with which to practice. That didn't happen in just a year, and other projects were undertaken and completed while the first two were being realized.

The enthusiasm resulted in an arena being approved, by all concerned, near what is now Meadow Park. The arena was marked out and the oak posts for arena, corrals, chutes and announcer's stand were all chopped down in Moonridge and hauled to the site. "Wild Bill" Betterly laid out a plan for the postholes, the holes dug with a borrowed posthole digger, the posts set in position and the general outline began to take shape—and it looked good. Up to that point there had been no cost incurred. Now wire and boards and hinges, et cetera, all had to be bought, but we got those goods at cost and less from local and member merchants. It wasn't quite as pretty as a classic arena in Cheyenne, but it was a labor of love and looked good to us. It fit the area, the times and our rodeos and ropings, as well as our finances. We purchased some calves, and practiced our roping on them.

Then came the important and predictable decision; to hold a full-scale rodeo every Fourth of July and every Labor Day. And we didn't have a dime. We had six or eight roping calves, and everyone had to come up with ideas, which had to be pretty good as there was no money to spend. So one member offered to obtain money for broncs by getting a donation of $40 from about a dozen or so merchants. One member, Buttons Dean, offered six or seven wet cows and their calves for the bell calf roping and the wild cow milking. Another member, Spence Cooper, offered his services as clown and bullfighter. A committee was formed to clean up, doll up, and improve the rustic appear-

87

ance of the arena by hiding some of it behind bright colored bunting. Several of the pretty girls were agreeable to passing the hat during the rodeo to collect a little expense money. The decision of the membership was to not charge admission, but just try to cover the absolutely necessary and unavoidable expenses, and that arrangement worked well for years.

Frank Bogert, Mayor of Palm Springs—who normally got $500 per day as a professional announcer—agreed to help our show as announcer for free. For free! And he was the best, a real plus for our rodeo. Art Manning, Sheriff's Captain at Barstow and former world champion bull rider, agreed to be the arena director and organize the parade from Red Ant Hill to the rodeo grounds—again for free!

A couple Vaqueros rode over to Holcomb Valley and got Bob Hitchcock, owner of the Y Double H cattle ranch and veteran cowman of the San Bernardino Mountains, to agree to be arena timer, flagman and race judge. He was willing, so convincing him was an easy task. Another plus for the show.

Mary Rose Stone, who had originally come up with the name Vaqueros de las Montanas, called Joc Ann Murray, who lived in Long Beach, but was at the time located in Pioneertown where she was doing her stunt riding act at a little punkin' rollin' there. Mary Rose drove down, met with her and her future husband, Dooley Newton, and they agreed to come to Big Bear to do her act at no expense to the Vaqueros. A really nice, handsome pair of kids, good riders with good horses, and Western as they could be. And thus we had added a great crowd pleasing act to our show.

So, the first Vaqueros rodeo was coming up. Whether the Fourth of July or Labor Day, who knows? That was a long time ago, 35 or 40 years. But we had events lined up to rival any rodeo anywhere, events no longer included in California rodeos.

It was agreed this show's contestants would be local cowboys of San Bernardino County and adjacent areas. No pros, no turtles, but working or former working cowhands only. This was patterned in part after the great and successful non-pro rodeos held in Victorville during the 1930's.

Just like the big-time of Madison Square Gardens, we started off with a grand, grand entry—horses flying, flags waving, colorful costumes shining— and then all lined up facing the stands, which this first year had approximately 250 seats. Parked cars and trucks and standing spectators filled every inch of the entire fence line, five to ten deep in places. There was not even standing room left, with several thousand in attendance—believe it or not! Being free and right in town helped a lot, and the parade drew them in also.

Then the colors were presented by Mary and Kendall Stone to the playing of the National Anthem, and the guests, celebrities and officials were introduced. The action got underway with the releasing of seven Hip O Ranch calves with seven small boys on them—and it rained boys around there! The yelling and horn blowing got the youngsters and the show off with a bang. It was a great spectator event.

The first scheduled event was saddle bronc riding. In this non-pro show some of them really stuck their heads in the dirt; the event was won by Bud Waite, an IS Ranch cowboy. In the calf roping, the times weren't world records, but Floyd Tidwell won it in 17 seconds. Wild cow milking was a favorite with the crowd, first, to see a cowboy manhandle a big 1,000 pound cow from on the ground, and second to see a cowboy run with his Coke bottle of milk the length of the arena to get to the judge and receive the time-ending flag. This event was won by Bill Betterly and myself. The cow almost wiped out Wild Bill, and the crowd was pulling for the cow. In this situation S.O.B. really does mean Sweet Old Bill.

The team roping was a favorite event then as it is now, and Floyd Tidwell and Ted Harvey won it with very respectable times, all of which made them hard to live with. The bareback broncs were crowd-pleasers as always, and some came off very hard. It was won by Pottsie Brown, a Stocker cowboy. The releasing of six loose calves all at once, and a seventh calf wearing a cowbell, drew the best response of the day. Bell calf roping with six riders and seven calves all running, riding and roping simultaneously—what a hairy event! The first to get a rope on the bell calf, after first roping and tying one of the loose calves, was the winner. When the storm, the dust, the noise and the excitement was over, the winner was Buttons Dean of the Stocker Ranch.

Next, Joe Ann Murray with her stunt horse—and Spence Cooper, his young son, and his ridiculous, trained mare—came into the arena at the same time. "Coop" just stood by as she made one spectacular run after another to much clapping, whistling and horn blowing encouragement. Her "Russian drag" was particularly spectacular at a full gallop. And then disaster and tragedy struck: Joe Ann's pants split from stem to stern, and she couldn't wait for the gate to be opened to let her out of the arena. However, she was a huge success and though everyone felt badly for her, it was a terrific climax to a great, great act. But she never would do it again for us. We certainly would have had to build more bleachers if she did.

Rest assured Coop, as "Dummy" in his clown clothes and make-up, and his son also made up as a clown, really kept the crowd in stitches during his act with that ridiculous old mare he had trained to do things no horse is expected or supposed to be able to do. Homer Holcomb and his mule didn't have a thing on Coop, and Holcomb got $800 a day for his act.

The bull riding was next, and there Cooper earned his money. What money? Anyway, he earned it even though he didn't get it. A crowd pleasing event that can be dangerous—what else pleases a crowd? It was won by Kendall Stone.

Now this show ran so smoothly and with no undue delays because the whole thing was so well orchestrated by the people in charge: Frank Bogert, Art Manning and Bob Hitchcock. No one can deny they were the best at their jobs. We couldn't have gotten better, or even as good, if we had spent a bundle to replace them. Frank Bogert is the only survivor of that trio.

The gymkhana events were used to fill in when the stock was being moved, sorted and replaced for action. These were fast, furious, and designed for the special purpose of keeping the crowd entertained. A pick-up race was run quickly with horses wide open while riders made flying mounts onto the running horses. The teams ran all at once and the winners were Kendall Stone and Mary Rose, though Buttons and Coop were only inches behind.

The wild or loose horse race, the other gymkhana event, is no longer used in rodeos or gymkhanas, since it's now considered too dangerous. It was run the entire circumference of the arena, with riders on loose horses—no saddle, no pad, no bridle, and no rope. They started at the chute end of the arena, and the first one back was the winner. Mary Stone was across the finish line first; she had lots of practice at this race in Palm Springs many years earlier. Dangerous? Yes!

With a warning over the loud speaker by Frank Bogert, admonishing everyone to drive carefully and soberly, the first Vaqueros rodeo wound down to a finish. We had collected enough money to pay for expenses and odds and ends, no one was seriously hurt, the spectators were happy and had enjoyed themselves, and the Vaqueros had successfully launched themselves on a career of one or two rodeos in Big Bear each year. The same riding club is still conducting this program of Western entertainment today.

The all-around silver buckle prize went to Floyd Tidwell; and just so you don't get the wrong impression, desert cowboys from Barstow, Needles, Victorville, Hesperia, and all points of the compass had successfully completed and won many points (dollars). These were to return in later years and give us even greater fits.

It is difficult to know why present-day rodeos do not have bell calf roping, loose horse races and wild cow milking. They are thought of highly by every cowboy, and all three are better, wilder and more interesting for spectators than almost any other events in the rodeo. I do not understand it: the only drawback I see is that in the one event you need wet cows, and rodeo promoters and stock contractors hedge away from that because of the added expense. They have come up with ribbon jerking, but really it's not the same. But even that is a more interesting and involved event than team roping, and much more action for the paying customers.

Talmadge cattle being worked in a corral near present-day Metcalf Bay, headquarters for the IS Ranch in the 1920's.

Chapter Twenty-Three

જ

Mountain Grizzlies Were Captured to Fight Bulls in Los Angeles

In the sleepy little Mexican settlement of El Pueblo de Nuestros Senora la Reina de Los Angeles, there was held for public viewing and betting, the several-thousand-year-old sport of bear and bull fighting. This was a particularly popular form of entertainment before and during California's gold rush days of the mid-19th century. The three necessary ingredients were a bear, a bull and a fairly spacious, sturdily built, adobe brick corral with high walls and strong gates. The bull and the corral were two readily available factors, but the third—the bear—was a horse of another color.

Dangerous to arouse, and difficult to handle, bears were never easy to obtain. Why? Because grizzly bears were used for this purpose and grizzlies were not known for being gentle, small or cooperative. The official nomenclature *Guigantus terriblus* was not adopted without merit! The grizzly's reputation fulfills its Latin genus hands down.

However, Mexican vaqueros did rope a grizzly on occasion, tie them up, or down (take your choice), place them on an oxen-drawn sled and transport them to the arena. But they never had enough grizzlies to meet the demand and so, since they paid cash money for the bears (and cash was mighty scarce) other enterprising, imaginative, cash-short persons also got into the act.

One for instance, was Francis (Frank) Lebaron Talmadge, my great-grandfather who encountered a number of these beasts when cutting timber for his saw mill in the 1860-1870's. And Frank Talmadge —sportsman, woodsman, hunter, scout and wagon boss that he was— came up with a way to relieve the ongoing shortage of cash, and have a little dangerous sport to go with it.

With the assistance of a couple of his mill hands he constructed a small log cabin with a stout floor and fashioned the door to be one entire end of the cabin. This would slide up and down, which thus became the trap door for a particularly large figure-4 trap. The trigger, as is customary for such figure-4 traps, was a large, flat board in the center of the trap (or cabin, in this case) upon which the bait would be placed. This was built in place but, although heavy, was movable. Then, the next step was taken when a beef or deer was killed for the mill crew. The head, hide and feet of this kill were tied together and then dragged (leaving hair, blood and scent) in a large circle of about a mile, down into the valley, out on to the meadow and up the hillside to the constructed cabin/trap. Here the dragged material, as well as the intestines, were thrown on and behind the trigger.

In some cases it was the same night, and in other incidents two or three days would pass before the trap would be sprung. If the catch were a small bear or a grizzly with cubs, or some other animal, it would be released. When the prize was a full-grown grizzly, the chore of loading the trap (the cabin itself) onto a heavy ox-drawn wagon would be accomplished, and, because time was of the essence, the trip down to San Bernardino and hence to Los Angeles was immediately begun. It might be added, the time period here was before the age of the railroad, so the entire procedure—covering less than 100 miles—usually required a whole week.

Upon arrival in Los Angeles, at the site of the big adobe corral, the bear would be sold to the Mexicans, and soon the bear was turned into the corral and then determined to be either big or average, male or female, fat or lean. With that completed the betting would begin. A bull would be obtained for the purpose of the fight, which would be held very soon after the bear arrived, maybe one or two days. The fights, of course, were bloody and noisy, and often prolonged, but eventually one would kill the other.

One big old she-grizzly taken from Little Bear to Los Angeles killed at least eight Spanish horned fighting bulls before succumbing to the wounds of the eighth and the fury of the ninth encounters. Supposedly, family history and handed down stories suggest that it was the fightingest grizzly ever to be used in Los Angeles. Descriptions of the fight itself were graphic: furious bursts of energy, fighting and sparring, with hide, hair, blood and dust flying every which way. Periods of calm would intersperse—when both animals on opposite sides of the corral would catch their breath and stare at each other—both probably wishing they could escape the corral. But soon the bear would growl and roar and stand upon its hind legs and the bull would face off and paw dirt and dust up over its back and they would return to mortal combat.

This would be repeated several times before one or the other would be mortally wounded and the fight concluded. The bets would then be paid off, the winner stared at admiringly and the loser skinned and cleaned with the meat given to the poor. This latter procedure is the practice today with bull fights in Mexico and Spain.

To our more delicate and, we think, compassionate tastes of today, this sport does seem unnecessarily cruel. But we must remember that those ancestors were living in a much more rugged era, where everything came harder. They worked longer and harder, played seldom but then did so all out—their games were rougher and the rules were not "Marquis of Queensberry"—and they loved " 'til death do us part." Most anything went, shootouts were not too common, but condoned to a much greater degree if fair and both men had equal chance. For instance, the knife fight between the Greek and the Chinaman in Holcomb Valley was just a way to settle an argument—both died.

So, maybe they did not have as great a compassion for all life that we like to pride ourselves with today, as it is popular to be compassionate about dogs, kids, whales, minnows, battered wives, the sick, the elderly, et cetera—just name anything living. But you have to admit that "compassion is the easy virtue," at least in these contemporary times. To say anything against compassion, conservationists, et cetera, is equated with being against "motherhood" and "apple pie."

Just as a final aside, it is interesting to note that since the dawn of time at least several million species of life have been extinguished. Yet modern society seems to be trying to reverse this, one in which I don't think we will be successful. We are also against erosion—any place at any time—and here again we are bucking nature, which really hasn't done so badly. Think about it: all the flat land, agricultural land, rich soil and loam is all—repeat, all—the result of erosion. So why are we trying to stop it?

I guess I've wandered enough—"Further deponent sayeth not."

Chapter Twenty-Four

ഇ

California Condors in the San Bernardino Mts.

Condors have been very much in the public eye recently, especially so as magazines, newspapers, radio and T.V. news, all make much out of the fact that the Condor now is a desperately endangered species. Reference is, of course, on the California Condor, which is found no where else on earth other than in certain parts of Southern California. The Pacific Coast of South America, and in particular Peru and Chile, still have respectful numbers of the South American Condor, a similar (yet different) cousin of our badly depleted California species.

There are a mere handful in captivity at the present time, and the effort to breed and raise them in confinement has met with little success. Scientists have carefully removed condor eggs from their nests, but that too has resulted in limited success; hatch, yes; survive, no. But science is endeavoring to rectify this, as attested by recurring reports on the evening news. Supposedly, there are five (ye gads, only five?) left in the wild, and one news report said they were all of one sex. If that's true, it is all over but the shouting. Too bad, for they were a magnificent creature of the sky. And, "believe it or not," they used to be plentiful in the San Bernardino Mountains.

John Wiley Talmadge, born in Little Bear (Lake Arrowhead) in 1864, remembered as a boy lying on his back in the meadow where the waters of Lake Arrowhead are today found, and seeing condors "stiff winged" soaring above him so high that occasionally they appeared as tiny specks. John would lie and watch them for long periods of time, either on the meadow or at the top of Strawberry Peak, where he and his brothers went frequently to get the goats that had gotten out of their corral at the sawmill. These goats, just like their wild ancestors and the modern big horns, wanted elevation so they could be above any predators that might be around, and upon escape they headed straightaway for the highest and closest peak. So it was on Strawberry Peak where John and brothers would find the wayward goats, and from there he'd watch the beautiful flight of the condors. May I repeat, observing the condors—either on a carcass or up high, high in the sky—was commonplace in those days.

Ultimately, when John Talmadge was a man with a family, he shot a condor with a wing spread of about nine feet, presented it to the Pioneer Society in San Bernardino, and it hung on the wall of the Society's old log cabin for many years until the building burnt down. I remember seeing it there, in the old log cabin, with its beautiful white distinctive underwing design when I was eight or nine years old. A little cloudy maybe, but I do remember it because Puppup showed it to me and told how he had shot it—not something a boy is apt to forget.

These huge birds were, of course, scavengers; awkward on the ground, ungainly while taking off, cumbersome when landing by a carcass, and disgusting and smelly in the way they ate and what they ate. Gorging themselves, truly gluttons when it was available, they would eat on a carcass—any and all of it—until they were almost aerodynamically kaput. But with a long run, a high leap and the use of the afterburner, they would finally become airborne. Once in flight, they were magnificent and beautiful, huge yet graceful in balance and so spectacular with a soaring freedom, something we'd all like to experience. Truly unique, these great birds are unequaled in the world of flight. They could and would soar for long periods of time without flapping their wings, using their unique eyesight and very special sense of smell to locate dead animals (carrion), which they could do from miles away.

Soaring and using thermals and updrafts, just like a modern glider, they stayed airborne for hours at a time, rising and smelling, circling and looking—a very special way of hunting. When they were low enough to see, Puppup said their white markings were very distinctive and noticeable, to which he joshingly explained, "you couldn't hardly mistake it for a hummingbird."

Well, the condor and the common buzzard, of which we still have a few to be seen upon occasion, did, it must be admitted, keep Southern California and the San Bernardino Mountains free of vermin, diseased and tainted carcasses, and other forms of bad smelling and unhealthy dead. Generally they are a more efficient clean-up crew than the much touted *homo-sapiens;* just think about it!

While we are thinking along the subject, what about the common buzzard? Doesn't look like anyone is worrying about them, but they too are disappearing. Really. When a boy and later a young man, I could count thousands of migrating buzzards in the Spring and Fall seasons, in their huge circling cones, drifting slowly over the desert and mountains, ridding the terrain of its dead like a vacuum cleaner. With literally thousands in a cone, itself several thousand feet from top to bottom, the cone of slowly circling buzzards moved north or south at a leisurely pace, not rushing on to some appointment like mankind seems to do. An unusual sight, to put it mildly—and one not seen in Southern California in many years.

So what's to do? Hey, I only write these stories, but will say with strong belief, the condor and the buzzard weren't "shot out" of the skies—they were "civilized out."

The author on 'Arkansaw' in the beautiful hi-desert country of Morongo Valley in 1985.

ოს

The Waterhole, Center of a Universe

In the desert, there is one place that is the "center of the universe" for those that live reasonably close by. These are the many springs—thousands in some areas—each of which serves as the center of a regional universe, in its own little location, with its own population.

I know! I know! There are desert dwellers that do not require the use of a spring of water to survive, and that is true; there are many millions of such inhabitants. They are among the few who get moisture from their food and the occasional desert rains. Turtles, kangaroo mice, lizards, some snakes—all can live their lives out away from and never see a permanent source of water. It is a neat trick and a gastronomical and natural balancing act that nature has provided some of its desert dwellers. Yet even in their unique way they are at extreme risk every time a drouth is experienced, for they too can, and do, die during such periods. Nothing can live without moisture. They just have special methods in making and storing it, and Mother Nature plays deadly tricks on them from time to time.

But of those who must take in moisture by mouth—and do so frequently in hot summer months—the desert spring, oasis, seep, damp spot, waterhole, or whatever name you choose to use, is (and again I repeat) the center of their universe. If you want to see the fauna and birdlife of the desert, take a pair of fieldglasses and find a lookout above and some distance from a desert spring. During the hot summer months almost every animal and every bird in the vicinity will come to drink, usually at least once every 24 hours. Birds by the score, as well as many large or small game and unique animals, can be seen.

You should choose a time when there is a full moon because much of the animal life is most apt to drink at night. But drink they will, unless you scare or annoy them, or hide where your scent will be carried in the direction of the water.

If you want to make it a particularly lucrative camera safari, place some salt blocks in the immediate area of the spring. This, of course, is a second, almost irresistable attraction for many animals. They drink usually quite quickly and, almost ghostlike, are then gone. However the salt will have the tendency to hold them for longer periods at the spot you have chosen, and this affords more time to watch, study, take photos, record sounds, shoot or whatever.

Bees, hornets, yellow jackets and wasps also must have moisture to make honey and comb, and if you are inclined toward these little critters, they too will be found in numbers at every place where there is water or even dampness. A myriad of mostly airborne insect life can also be expected around water on the desert. I never remember looking at a spring or waterhole on the desert, winter or summer, without seeing insect life, flying life, crawling life, slithering life, and so on.

Every desert carnivore is acutely aware that life centers around water in his world. A good place to find rabbits, squirrels, rats, etc., is around the water. And many, even though not thirsty, frequent the area because it is the center of life there. It is a good place to find one's breakfast, lunch, dinner, or even a midnight snack. The carnivore is not worried about overeating. Freedom from pumping iron, fighting a spare tire, following a diet, or having to refuse a second piece of pumpkin pie, goes with the territory.

All roads lead to Rome? I guess so. I followed one most of the way from Anzio to Rome (during WWII), and on foot, too. The road did go to Rome all right, but the only place I wanted to go was home—to the San Bernardino Mountains and the Mojave Desert. Never did they look or sound so good as when I was in Europe. Those poor folks over there didn't even speak English, or know who won the World Series or that the Alamo and Bastogne have a lot—a whole lot —in common.

I guess you never know which way this pen is going to go; but just as it is a true statement that all roads lead to Rome (at least the Italians of old thought so, rightfully), so it is that all bird and insect flightways and all carnivore and herbivore fauna trails lead to water in the desert. Try following one! Of course you can't go toward Sicily from Naples and get to Rome, just as you can't go towards feeding areas from wherever you hit the trail.

All of them, however—game trails, quail trails, etc.—will go to the water if you follow them in the right direction, and they will always follow the easiest grades and go through the lowest passes that offer the least resistance. Natural trails that are made by horses, burros, deer, etc., are interesting studies of design and can even provide "book learned" engineers a bit of knowledge from time to time.

For instance, Uncle Will Talmadge took the state road engineers (who eventually built the high-gear road) on horseback from the dam to Lake View Point on an old cow trail. And I have to give them credit—they followed that old Indian, game, cattle, horseback trail almost exactly. It is an engineering marvel and model which seldom, summer or winter, gives any real trouble—maybe a few snow slides, a few rock slides—but one thing is certain: you are responsible to keep your car on it, and if you don't, it can be hazardous to your health.

The desert springs plus an occasional stream and some windmills are what hold together innumerable cow ranches in the deserts of the Southwest. They are the glue that allows it all to happen. Millions of pounds of beef are raised for human consumption on the Mojave Desert, and each cattleman and cowpuncher would freely admit that without ownership of or legal access to many springs, this source of vital protein and energy would and could not exist. Tens of thousands of dollars are involved.

You think cattlemen know only about cows? They do know a bunch about cows. You think cattlemen know only about cows and horses? They do know a lot about cows and horses. You think cattlemen know only about cows and horses and graze? They do know about those things—cattle and their care and breeding; horses and their care and breaking and training; graze—a cowman can wax eloquent at the drop of a hat when you talk of tall grass, graze, browse, chaparral, locoweed and on and on.

But did you ever see a desert cattleman at work on a spring or seep or damp spot on the sidehill up some little old canyon on the Mojave? No? Well, you ain't lived yet. To start with, his lore is replete with tales of miners, homesteaders, sandlappers, dudes, Easterners, and particularly persons who arrived here from areas and countries where water was in great abundance.

The tales dealt with the total loss of the water from many springs where someone, in some dang hurry, would drill a three to six foot deep hole (of small diameter) at a spring, seep or damp spot, stuff the hole with dynamite and expect to instantly double or triple the flow, or maybe strike an artesian. Who knows? It sounds great. But sadly—and almost invariably—the explosion would break up the fragile rock or clay that was forcing the water to the surface, and the almost universal result was the total loss of water. A good little spring was lost forever.

With that little tidbit of wisdom working for him, you wouldn't believe the sneaky, careful, delicate, loving way a cowman would treat such a source of water with a shovel, a pick, a bar, a camel's hair brush—naw, I'm just kidding about the camel's hair brush. But very delicately and slowly he would pick and shovel his way into the clay bank or whatever, following the damp, wet strata. Seems like just a tiny bit more water or dampness, pretty soon a few feet further real mud is encountered; dig a little depression, form a little dam and go eat his crackers and sardines for lunch and sure enough, upon his return there was a little puddle of dirty water. A few more bites with the pick, a few more shovelsful moved, and water can be seen seeping out of the side of the cut and running openly down to a little pool rapidly forming in the bottom of the cut—five feet deep and 15 feet back into the bank.

By next morning it wasn't just a good little pool, but some water was slowly easing down the cut. The pool was running over. Then many different things were done. A barrel was sunk into it to catch the water, or a little dam was built to make the pool bigger and deeper. Perhaps a pipe with window screening over the end would be run up into the pool, and the water would run down several sections of pipe to a trough made of iron, cement, wood, or just clay.

Now the source had to be fenced to keep the cattle, horses, burros, and deer from tromping it out, and the pipeline sturdied up so it could not be damaged by animals stepping on or over it. Then you showed it to a half-dozen old cows and calves and introduced it to a bull or two, and you had perhaps just opened another 10 square miles of good grazing land benefiting cattle, game, quail, chucker and dove as well as many other desert creatures and varmits.

Building up springs is to real cattlemen as chess may be to certain other members of the *homo sapiens*. It's fun, it's outdoors, it's tricky, it's profitable when successful, and it's a challenge. I must here add, chess is not a good simile—it's much more than that, as any thirsty old mortgage-lifting mother cow can readily see.

I certainly have to admit here and now there are at least a thousand variations on the development of a waterhole in the desert. Each is unique in its own right. Each cattleman handles it differently, many times depending on just how much water is developed. They do not normally try for a hundred miner's inches of water—a small fraction of a miner's inch would do very handily.

There is no intention of planting and irrigating a 50-acre plot of alfalfa. That only happened once, and that is well known. It is exactly the way Old Woman Springs water was developed, and Al Swarthout planted, irrigated and harvested a large acreage of alfalfa from one such seep or spring that had been an old Indian camp on the Mojave Desert. His success and water turned out to be available through a siphon system that he could turn off and on at will. He and Charlie Reche did it with a pick and shovel—no camel's hair brush, but rest assured they were careful not to be violent enough to lose it.

Reche then homesteaded about 12 or 15 miles S.E. He dug a well on the same fault as Old Woman and got water standing in his well at about 25 feet. Talmadge Bros. IS cattle ranch used that well in conjunction with Charlie Reche for many years. It opened up 50 square miles of grazing, of which the cattle could much more readily take advantage, especially in very warm weather.

"Just out east of Surprise."

"Go by and clean out Saddle Rock first time you're over that way."

"I'll meet you about noon at Mound."

"I saw three cows and calves at Bulls--t; go by and move them to Bryant at your first opportunity."

"Drive that big red-cheeked bull at One Horse back to White-water tomorrow."

What?!! Every cowboy and cattleman in this end of the country knew exactly to what and where you were referring. One Horse, Bryant, Bulls--t, Mound, Saddle Rock and Surprise are all springs of good year-round water on the cattle range in that big area. The country and area was often and very normally identified by the name of the nearest water. They were as easily identifiable to the local cattle ranchers as "Meet you at Hollywood and Vine" is to the residents of Los Angeles.

The relationship between desert flowers and plants were very much appreciated by the desert aborigines. For instance:

Beavertail cactus: The seeds, pods, buds and fruit were all eaten.
Paloverde: Seeds were a source of food for Indians.
Encelia: Indians smeared the resin on for pain.
Screwbean mesquite: Pods were eaten by cattle; Indians pounded them
    into meal and made cakes of an edible tortilla-like configuration.

Prickly Poppy: Seeds were used by Indians as a narcotic.

Chia: Seeds were widely gathered for food; contained very high protein (known as Indians' iron rations).

Manzanita: Seeds were pounded into a meal to make mush.

Yerba santa: Leaf tea used for coughs.

Squaw cabbage: Young stems boiled with meat to make a stew.

Desert lily: Bulbs used to flavor food.

The Indians used some part of almost every plant, bush or tree on the desert for some purpose. Their thousands of years of residence here had allowed them to find out about and take advantage of many items that the uninitiated would find no possible use for.

The white man still finds no use for many of the things that the Indian found good, palatable, useful or gourmet. Often though, narcotic or stupifying properties of plants were used in religious ceremonies, i.e., prickly poppy, peyote, datura and saguaro cactus. Other parts of plants made clothing items, sandals, shades, mats, baskets, wickiups, leantos, arrow shafts, bows, spears, carrying bags, cosmetics, and even war paint.

Speaking of desert springs as important centers of the universe may sound far-fetched, but as a matter of fact, each of the thousands of springs in the Mojave Desert is a center of life and livelihood and even death and propagation for its dwellers, thousands upon thousands of them.

So if you want to actually see, instead of attempting to visualize, an independent world with your very own eyes, try an extended visit to a year-round spring and its immediate surrounding hundreds of acres. See for yourself a "world-of-its-own" in operation—one which has probably been in operation for countless years and still remains much the same with a very similar population to what it had 10,000 years ago. Each is still in its little niche of survival, life and death, just as it was long before the birth of Christ.

And it has the same flying, creeping, crawling, walking, slithering, hopping inhabitants.

Chapter Twenty-Six

ᘓᘏᘍ

Springtime in the Desert

Springtime in the desert: there are not enough adequate words in any language to do justice to the season of spring in the Mojave Desert. It can be a wonderland with a profusion and mixture of flowers, grass, browse, brush, chaparral, willows, and wash willows; cottonwoods, oaks, pinons, cacti, yuccas, Joshuas and palms; all in their glory and beauty, each different from the other and each more startling.

There are at least three kinds of desert springs. First, the normal spring, which is beautiful and outstanding, interesting and worth a long trip just to enjoy for sightseeing, picnicking and hiking.

Secondly, there is the dry, droughty spring which is not frequent, but you can depend on a few of them to be mixed in. The desert flora and fauna seem to cease to exist; range cattle can starve to death; the year-round springs go dry; the water table falls; the worst of these springs sees the death of even some cacti. Everything draws into itself with survival its only thought. Even the cactus that survives, and most of it does, shrivels up and uses all of its stored moisture. Parts of bushes and parts of some trees die so the rest of the growth might survive. These are the periods between winter and summer that are dreaded by man and beast as well as all plant life.

Coming out of winter, everything has been kind of holding its breath anyway, waiting for the spring rains and warm weather that heralds the growing, sprouting, birthing, bearing season. When the moisture fails, it becomes evident that the warmth of spring alone is not sufficient and only harkens the treachery of a hot desert summer. That season then comes without the benefit of the rains, coolness and runoffs of a spring which normally allows decent growth and animals to have a good start into the long hot summer months.

Finally, we find the occasional (not infrequent) spring of abundance, unbelievable abundance. Even having watched, gloried in, appreciated and doted on such springs for a lifetime, no one is ever ready for, nor hardly able to believe, a spring that arrives after the winter and spring rains come. Not necessarily a tremendous wet and rainy spring, but one in which the rains (even fairly light rains) come at the proper times, spaced correctly for maximum growth of the desert flora. Every other thing—insect, carnivore, herbivore, bird-life, crustacean and reptile—all depend totally on the green spring growth.

For instance, and it may not be universally known, the quail population will, on a spring such as we are describing, have large coveys of young and might even have two hatchings. And the antithesis—during a dry spring where the male quail doesn't get an abundance of fresh, tender, green growth to eat, his semen will not make fertile the whole clutch of eggs his mate will lay, and the coveys will be small; amazing, but a built-in safeguard of nature not to propagate more than it can feed.

Nature's subtle and not-so-subtle touches in the desert dictate life and death, growth and decay. The desert seems tough, and in many ways it is, but also it has a very fragile balance which can be devastated by man-made travesties when these are added to the natural terrors in such a temperamental, playful, changing environment.

But the metamorphosis of the desert is really magic and like witchcraft during these special springs that astound and dumbfound. They are absolutely unbelievable, making you at least figuratively bow down to a greater being to see nature at its best and most spectacular. Everything grows, everything greens up, everything blooms, everything bears and hatches and breeds and propagates—a cornucopia of abundance, causing harvests of pinons, acorns, cactus apples, wild cherries and plums.

Flowers, flowers, flowers everywhere. There will be large acreage where a man cannot step down on less than five to 10 plants and flowers—millions and billions of blooms as far as the eye can see. This is perhaps the most spectacular and noticeable item of such a bountiful spring. No artist and no paint can even begin to do justice to this vista of color that rolls on for miles and miles. Yellow, red, blue, green, purple, each are present in 20 shades, some harsh reds and brilliant yellows but mostly muted, delicate, inbetween shades of subtle color—and frequently acres of it.

There are believed to be 1500 varieties of wild flowers on the desert, many with only subtle differences. For the most part those are only very interesting to scientifically inclined persons—for you and me it is enough that we see the beauty. Lives there a man with soul so dead that he is unable to see and appreciate the glory of it?

These enormously productive springs cause alot of stir and growth in many other things besides flowers. The very rocks appear to be affected. And at the very least the beauty is reflected in, on and around them when beauty and greenery is in such profusion. The rocks are made more becoming by the presence of all the flora and fauna in their most beautiful finery, flowers, feathers and fur. And rocks with petroglyphs and pictographs on them also are framed and set off spectacularly by the unusual color of poppy, cacti, mallow and sage blooms bursting right out of the cracks in the rocks.

The Indians shared in these abundant times. Everything was easier, greener, wetter. Men, women and particularly children grew fat and sleek; living was easy and game abundant. Prosperity in those times depended almost entirely on nature, mostly activated by the spring rains which occurred at the right times.

In more recent times the wonder of such lush periods was strikingly shown in another way. The big old range cows that ran on the deserts found a good living too. Their calves were larger and grew faster and they themselves were fatter and happier than usual. (What was that about "contented cows"?)

At any rate two or three old cows started toward the high meadows from the desert on one such spring. Followed by their pretty little white-faced calves walking slowly up a trail from Reche's Well toward Painted Rock, the abundance became almost painfully apparent. The old cows' full bags were dripping milk with every step. The calves had so much they could not drink it all.

On these springs the old mother cows, the mortgage-lifters, would be so big and fat and heavy that they had to be brought off the lower sandy deserts, because their added weight would force their toes deep into the overheated sands (starting in April). The tender skin between the toes would be blistered and raw and cause the cow to go very lame. If an old cow were left there a few days too long, she would become so lame that she'd be unable to walk on to the high, cool mountain meadows where she was supposed to summer.

That was one of the many jobs of the cowboys who wintered on the desert with the cattle—get them out of the low, hot, sandy country before the big old mother cows were incapacitated. This was aggravated, of course, by the fact that the water hole, spring or windmill might be five or more miles from the areas the cows fed in.

These are the years when the extra trillions of seeds from every living plant on the desert are broadcast wholesale in and on the thousands and thousands of square miles of the Mojave Desert and the adjacent foothills. You could mark off a 10 or 20 foot square almost anyplace on the desert and foothills, and in the winter it will be sand, dirt, rock, gravel, etc. But even then the birds—quail, dove, wild pigeons, Western bluebirds, swallows, wrens, thrushes, chukars, thrashers, etc.—will scratch, find and consume thousands of seeds from your small plot (what a dead, uninteresting-looking place to the uninitiated). But come a good spring, hundreds of plants in many varieties will almost jump from the ground in the spot that was picked at random.

The coyotes, bobcats, kanagroo mice, pack rats, rattlesnakes, cottontails and jack rabbits all get fat and sleek on the over-abundance pressed upon them by the very same Mother Nature who just a year earlier starved half of them to death. Who said, "fickle female"?

Old-timers swear that on such a spring you can stop and get off your horse in a real lush little green vale, and by lying down and being real still and paying special attention, you can actually hear the filaree growing. Well, I don't know about that, but corn belt people from back East swear you can go into a cornfield and hear the corn growing, so why not filaree? I guess you can't really, but it makes a good story.

A springtime in the desert can, I am sure, do as much to combat atheism as all the churches' best efforts, bless them! "Oh puny man who cannot create a single miracle, fashion one bud, or throw one cloud into a sunny sky—how dare you doubt the only One who can."—*Anon.*

Everyone dwelling on or acquainted with the desert can tell, even foretell to some degree, what kind of a spring the upcoming one will be. These wet springs bring to flower all of the drought evaders who do not blossom, or at least not so profusely, as in these ideal years. It can be referred to as "birth control"; and they seem to know how much rain is needed to see them through their short life. But even on the most ideal spring only parts of the seeds of some plants will germinate. Some stay dormant in case of emergency and are a reserve for a later time, should it be needed.

Nowhere on earth is there anything like the riotous abandon of color in Southern California (for example: miles of poppies near Bakersfield; miles of verbena near Palm Springs and the miles and vistas of encelia on a sympathetic spring).

The flowers? I'm glad you asked, but it is bewildering to try and guess where to start.

Desert Mallow: Deep apricot to bright red.

Indian Paintbrush: The bracts are brilliant red, the flowers inconspicuous.

Beavertail Cactus: Magenta to orchid flowers.

Hedgehog Cactus: Rose to purple flowers.

Firecrackers: Scarlett flowers with long stems.

Mojave Asther: Violet to white with yellow centers; many flowers on each plant.

Desert Rattleweed: Pea family; reddish purple.

Scarlett Locoweed: Pea family; bright scarlett.

Ocotillo: Up to 20 feet tall; brilliant red blossoms.

Sand Verbena: Purplish rose-colored flowers; almost solid ground cover for miles.

Manzanita: Heath family; delicate pink flowers.

Wild Rhubarb: Buckwheat family; pinkish blossom.

Squaw Tea: Joint fir family; leaves are tiny scales; flowers are nondescript, a harsh stingy perennial; makes a refreshing drink when dried and boiled like tea; also called Mormon Tea, Indian Tea.

Mariposa Lily: Lily family; many colored flowers.

Rose Sage: Blue flowers; mint family.

Paper Bag Bush: Mint family; white flowers.

Arrow-weed: Sunflower family; pale purple flower; Indians used the stems to make arrows.

Mojave Locoweed: Pea family; rose purple; cattlemen's enemy.

Rose Desert Lupine: Pea family; blue or purple.

Great Basin Blue Sage: Mint family; blue flowers; similar to purple sage of Texas.

Smoke Tree: Pea family; blue-purple flower.

Larkspur: Crowfoot (buttercup) family; light to deep blue.

Chia: Mint family; blue flower; seeds gathered by the Indians to be used as "iron rations".

Desert or Wash Willow: Begonia family; white, pink, lavender flowers; known also as the orchid tree.

Desert White Astor: Sunflower family.

Chuparosa: Acanthus family; dull red flower; hummingbirds probe for both insects and nectar.

Prickly Poppy: Poppy family; white flowers; seeds are narcotic—more narcotic than opium.

Others are:
*Dune primrose, yucca, Joshua, cliff rose, Apache plume, desert holly, Death Valley locoweed, cliff aster.
*Desert gold poppy, California dodder, screwbean, mesquite, coyote melon, jojoba, desert plume, catsclaw.
*Greasewood, encelia, palo verde, desert trumpet, burro-brush, desert marigold, yellow nightshade.

This is only a small sample of the many flowers and plants, brush and chaparral of the desert areas. There is also a whole family of "belly-flowers," so small that a person has to lie down on his stomach to see them well.

The author at age nine, on John Talmadge's top horse 'Pinto', which he was allowed to ride in the Big Bear Fourth of July 1928 Parade. "You couldn't touch me with a ten-foot pole, I was so proud."

Chapter Twenty-Seven

ᏫᏫ

Rattlesnake Canyon Winds Down to the Desert

Rattlesnake Canyon: big, long, deep, varied, useful, extensive, running from high to low, from cold and snow to heat and sand. The canyon is home to a multitude of wildlife and vegetation from pines to pinon to cholla, all of which could lead you to agree that Rattlesnake Canyon is a great statement even for Mother Nature to make. It can be explored on foot or horseback, and a hint of what it has to offer can be gleaned by motorists traveling Pioneertown Road.

When you describe a canyon, just as when you discuss a river, you must start at the beginning. Just as the Nile, the longest river in the world, has two starting places or sources—the Blue Nile and the White Nile—so, too, does the beautiful long canyon that goes from 7,000 feet to the desert floor.

The two starting places of Rattlesnake Canyon in the eastern San Bernardino Mountains are the Round Valley and Rose Mine areas above the Golden Stairs. Just after the junction of these two, about a third of a mile down, the water and trail pass through the Needle's Eye, a place where the Talmadge Brothers' IS cattle and the Swarthout Heart Bar cattle were always counted, because only one cow-brute could pass through at a time.

Will Talmadge could be seen on Old Blue, Buddy or Spelick, sitting on the side hill above the Needle's Eye, to get an accurate count on what was going into the high meadows, for decade after decade, starting back in the 1880's.

Just below the Golden Stairs and just above the Needle's Eye is the junction of the two starting sources. Here, under big old cottonwoods and near an old rock dugout is the location of an old Spanish arrastre. Some rocks used are still to be seen, but no actual arrastre is there at this time. In the 1920's much of it and its machinery were plainly seen beside a little spring. Presumably, this arrastre prepared the ore for the smelter located another mile down the canyon.

Tributaries? Yes, there are scores. One of the first comes down through the old tungsten mine area, goes directly in front of Bill Kramer's old Sleepy Hollow homestead and a hundred yards past, then empties into Rattlesnake. At this point, the east-flowing canyon turns northeast and goes to Mound Springs where the water comes right out of a large mound of dirt. Here was good water for cattle, game and birds 12 months of the year, and one of Swarthout's Heart Bar corral and camping areas. From there the canyon turns generally almost north, but winds and twists just like a rattlesnake for about 12 miles, passing many tributaries on both sides, including Burro Canyon which has a good trail going up it to Duncan Flat. In the main canyon the water raises and runs various distances several times during that 12 miles—good water for game and cattle; and many mountain quail coveys inhabit this area of the canyon.

As you continue on down, there are several side canyons that have spilled alluvial fan debris into the canyon itself. In one instance in the last few years the debris closed off the canyon and it formed a lake several acres in size and several feet deep. The evidence of its filling up and breaking over the top and tearing out one side of the erstwhile dam is still there and easy to read. That particular summer thunderstorm was a gully washer and lots of terra firma changed locations, and it was plain to see that boulders the size of a pickup truck had been rolled, moved and crashed against each other for a further distance than seemed realistic.

Almost to the mouth of the canyon is Rattlesnake Spring, a large trough and damp, grassy runoff area. It's a superior permanent watering place for cattle, deer, bear, quail, dove, and all other bird life and all varmits of the area, including coyotes, bobcats, and mountain lions.

In 1939, two cowboys had arrived at Rattlesnake Spring in the hot afternoon after gathering and driving cattle all day. Hot and dusty, they and their horses got a welcome cool drink, and the horses' saddles were pulled off to allow their backs to dry and cool off. While resting, talking and smoking, they heard, from almost a hundred yards away on the far side of the canyon in a rocky area, a rattlesnake sing, stop, and sing again. After several repetitions of the sounds, they became very curious. Rattlesnake Canyon, Rattlesnake Spring—it only figures there was a real, live rattlesnake buzzing, but from so far away it was not possible that these two horsemen had so aroused it.

They saddled their horses and rode over toward the sound. When they got quite close, that grizzly (rattlesnake) really sounded off. As they caught sight of it they could hardly believe their eyes. A big old she-grizzly was giving birth to a whole handful of little ones which were squirming around, crawling a little distance from her—probably a once-in-a-lifetime sight and experience. No one counted them, but probably by killing the old grizzly and all the newborn and even some not yet born, these two cowboys eliminated more poisonous snakes in less time and with less effort than anyone in history.

If you stand high on a hill on the edge of the canyon and look up and down its varied wonders for several miles, you could truthfully say, "That's a serious and staggering piece of God's business." And when you have ridden horseback for a whole day from the top to the bottom of the canyon you might very well opine, "I'm glad I have seen, for once, something there's enough of."

About a half mile after you pass Rattlesnake Spring, the canyon opens out onto the desert, and in floodtime the water can and does flow much further (miles and miles) out into the desert and into big, normally dry lakebeds. The actual canyon now is passed and the journey is completed—but in retrospect it has been a series of interesting views and findings. You couldn't have spent a day any better or more profitably than touring one of the seven wonders of the San Bernardinos.

The canyon does have its practical side too, having raised literally thousands of tons of beef over the last 100 years. That is to its credit.

Now, as to mining, it is an oft-heard saying among all the old-timers that much more gold and silver has been put into the ground of the San Bernardinos than ever was taken out of it. True, there were a few rich strikes—Holcomb Valley and Rose Mine are two—but countless thousands of mines, holes, tunnels, mill sites, dry washes, mining claims, and inumerable dollars and hours of labor were spent on proving up on nothing. However, miners are a strange, hardheaded, hard-working group who never give up and never say die, and it is truthfully certain that: one, gold is where you find it, and two, there are more rich strikes to be made. Where and when and by whom is the unanswered question.

n earth-filled embankment provides a dam for this desert spring, located near
Wood Canyon—just east of Duncan Flat. This
served as a waterhole for cattle and game.

Shay's Corral at Baldwin Lake is the scene for this 1947 dehorning. The autho: (in white shirt) and Tommy Davis secure the cow while Buttons Dean completes the chore.

ary and Kendall Stone at the San Bernardino County Sheriff's Annual Rodeo
committee meeting in 1962.

With the author on bay horse at left and grandson Ion Talmadge Stone on palomino in foreground, the family continues

Chapter Twenty-Eight

ᴄᴡᴏ

Cow Tracks: aka Readin' Sign

Tracking has become a game, but it was not always so. Although there are places where cattlemen still work, one way or another, all year around with cow-tracks, it is becoming a lost art. There are some pamphlets, articles and books on tracks and tracking; that is, how to tell a fox track from that of a coyote or a dog; a lion from a leopard and so on. However, this little treatise will confine itself to, for the most part, cowboys and cow tracks. It may not seem like it, but that combination, cowboys and cow tracks, are a very important part of the beef industry. Maybe not to the meat packer, the feed lot operator or the cattle buyer, but it is important to the cowman who is running cattle on the open range; whether mountain, foothill, prairie or desert. The proper expertise in "reading sign" is a job that only comes with many years of experience; you don't learn it from a book, you have to do it, see it, watch an old hand at work, listen to what he says, ask questions and most of all, observe. And as with most everything, you must have the desire to do it and do it well, and be willing to spend the time and effort to so do.

Is the knowledge vital? Yes, just as important as the ability to ride and rope. Is it an area of pride? Yes, to be a good or the best tracker and sign reader on the ranch is a plum every hand would be proud to have. Is the knowledge used frequently? Yes, daily on a ranch—it is at the least an important daily newspaper of happenings on the open range.

Who cares about the daily comings and goings of the loose stock? For one, the owner; and a good hand can tell him a great deal about his cattle from observations on a day's ride out onto the range. What can he tell? To name a few: how many cattle are in the area; are there any new calves; are the cattle well scattered or running in large bunches; are dog packs harassing the stock; how often are they watering; what feed is good, and what are the cattle eating at that time; are the bulls scattered throughout the range, or are they bunched up and living like a bunch of happy bachelors and consequently producing few calves. And really, much more—you may not see very many cattle on a big winter open range but you will see many tracks that can tell you a great deal, warn if they are doing well or in trouble over water, feed, varmits, campers, etc.

That specifically is the every day ongoing usage of tracking knowledge, but also, signs are absolutely vital when you go on the "rodear" (to gather) in the Spring. The cattle in the warm Spring weather must water every day or two, so cannot be too far from water. To gather them, you go to each waterhole, windmill, spring, etc., and track the little bunches out. On finding them, you drive them to the nearest corral or holding field 'till everything is gathered for the purpose of moving the cattle to the Summer range for branding, cutting, ear marking, vaccinating and dehorning as well as checking all stock for wounds, disease and tending to same, separating the beef steers, etc.

Another use of cow-trackers is the finding, tracking, roping and capturing of wild cattle. Wild cattle are seldom found without the use of "reading sign" and tracking, and if they should happen to be found otherwise, you will still have to use your tracking abilities at some point in the game. It is a game—a game that cowpunchers who are "hands" look forward to. In fact, it has always and often been said that the fact that there are wild cattle which need to be handled is one of the main reasons that cowboys will work for the proverbial "30 and found," i.e., thirty dollars a month and your room and board. When you jump a bunch of wild cattle or even one, it makes older men young again and makes the young mens' blood pump faster. The inherent danger and excitement have led to the adage, "if life is not an adventure, it is nothing."

Now you are in the country where the wild cattle are known to be and you (or several of you) are there for the express purpose of getting some of the wild cattle for perhaps several reasons. First, they are worth good money if you can capture and get them to a meat buyer. Second, they tend to make any gentle, profitable type cattle wild just by being with them—they run off when you approach, and the gentle cattle too will run under those circumstances, and then they can get hot and runny and hard to handle. Third, if the cattlemen and cowboys know of a few old mossyhorns running way back in the hills and canyons, they frequently go there and camp for a few days with good horses and camp grub. They do so mostly for the sport and fun, the danger, profit and competition, and to see who can tell the biggest windy around the evening campfire in regards to that day's tracking, chasing, catching, tying up, etc. (or if not that day's, maybe another chase three years ago.) After the steaks, Dutch oven biscuits and gravy and canned peaches have been consumed, a little bourbon and branch water just sets the day, the time, and the atmosphere off to a "T". As each checks his horse, waters and feeds him again and turns in, tired, but exhilarated in anticipation of tomorrow's adventure, he swears to himself that the next time he tracks down or jumps that big brindle steer with the crooked horn, he'll get him if he has to chase him clear to Texas.

When tracking, you often have to dismount to better interpret the tracks and sign. In rocky, hard ground, it's a challenge. Sometimes the same tracks that look fresh in damp earth, look a week old 20 feet further in the dry—you have to know which to believe. Also, you must find where cattle have bedded down. When they get up, the first thing each of them will do is deficate. This is very tell-tale if you properly interpret it, so how do you tell? First, look at it, then step on it, note how hard, how soft, how thick the crust, taking into consideration the heat, cold, or sunshine. Then feel of it, smell of it, and if necessary, it has been said a real professional will have all the knowledge available from that cow-pie just as soon as he has tasted it.

And what do you read into all these tracks and pies and heat and dampness, etc.? Well, when they are all put together in a mile or so (sometimes much less), they will reveal to you: age of tracks, when there, direction of travel, speed, doing which, going where, big stock, little, calf, bull, yearling, and are they going to water, feeding, running, trotting, playfully carousing, bulls pawing, which perhaps indicates two bulls(?). Tracks in sand, snow, dew, deep or thick grass, and mud are all different and must be interpreted and evaluated differently, a job for a cowboy who has done it all his life.

Then we could go off into tracking lost kids, wanted and escaped criminals, cougar, bear, deer, and other critters and varmits large and small, but that will have to wait for another time.

Cow tracks are as familiar to a cow puncher as his hat and as necessary as his horse—and a real cowranch cannot be properly, profitably and professionally ran without the knowledge of "readin' sign."

Chapter Twenty-Nine

ᔕᘯ

Swallow Nests Proliferate in Some Old Pines

In the Big Bear, Holcomb Valley and Baldwin Lake areas are some very special huge old pines doing extra duty above and beyond the norm for such old giants of the San Bernardinos. Always the biggest trees in their areas, mostly with spike tops, these were probably already big at the time Don Benito (Ben Wilson) stumbled onto our paradise on earth, Big Bear Valley.

These old fogies are almost always on the edge of a large, green, damp open meadow, such as China Garden meadow, Metcalf Bay Meadow, Shay's Meadow, Hitchcock's Meadow in Holcomb at the Y-double-H Ranch summer headquarters (a Boy Scout camp now), near the Erwin Lake Meadow, Upper Holcomb (near Hangman's Tree), and elsewhere that the right conditions prevail. These very special trees, besides being monarchs of the mountain, postcard beautiful ancient residents and outstanding denizens of their areas, are host to birds, squirrels, chipmunks and other wee varmits. But their real claim to fame is the annual spring return of the swallows, known also as mud daubers.

These beautiful little aerial acrobats return yearly to their same certain trees, just as they do to Capistrano, and just as predictably. Sometimes when the old greybeards fall, the birds have to find a new tree for their homes, but there are swallow trees in the Big Bear area which have had these residents every year for more than 60 years.

These glossy little flyers are bird engineers just as beavers are known as animal engineers; and they don't just have a masters degree, they have a doctorate in mud engineering. This they aptly demonstrate by finding the exact place to build, under big limbs where they connect to the tree, and also under the eaves of your house, for example. This keeps them from becoming wet and washed away in a summer thunderstorm. And what to build them of? It takes mud and water properly mixed, like the exact mixture necessary for cement. Then

116

they carry it in their beaks to the chosen spot and daub it against the bark, wood, cement or whatever, and it takes hundreds of such trips to build their beautiful little form-fitting nests, safe from rain and safe way up in the big old pines from almost everything else that might be inclined to harm the nest, the eggs, the baby birds or the parents.

An oddity—and also an old wives' tale—was the belief that these flying artists could not land on the ground, because in so doing they could not take off again. This belief was strengthened by the fact that their mud nests are built in the trees in such a way that they usually fly almost straight up and into the entrance, an acrobatic maneuver worth a circus billing. On exit they just turn loose and drop out of the long narrow entrance, frequently falling several feet before taking hold of the air and gracefully recovering.

When you find an area where they are picking up mud, sometimes there will be 20 or more at one time hovering over the soft muddy areas, or they may be seen skimming over the water, swooping down and picking up beakfuls of water so that the mud, the water and their little magic saliva are all firmed up into "swallow cement" for use on their nest, which they most usually have to completely rebuild each spring.

A sight to behold is when you see a number of them over a muddy area by a creek or lake, all hovering off the ground, the whole movement closely resembling a quaking aspen tree in a little breeze—and this, together with the manner in which they come and go from the nest, has given to posterity the old wives' tale. But they can take off from the ground, because if the area where they are picking up the mud is closely watched, occasionally one will be seen coming to rest and then taking off—not frequently, but it does happen. But it is very observable that they prefer to hover, for their own good reasons, I suspect.

Formerly the old-timers could tell almost the day they would arrive, and that a day or two prior the "scouts" would arrive to test the air, trees, mud and whatever—or maybe they just flew too fast. *Quien sabe?* It really would be an excellent project for perhaps, the Boy Scouts, the U.S. Forest Service, the historical society or just some interested citizen who knows the whereabouts of one such tree to begin an official calculation of their arrival, the scouts' arrival, and the date of their leaving. Look at San Juan Capistrano—it reaps a million dollars worth of publicity each year—why not Big Bear? For my money, these high altitude birds are much superior to the sea-level flatlanders. Ask anyone who flies an airplane if it's not more difficult to take off, fly and land at 7,000 feet—takes more skill and expertise and a bigger motor (lungs). And you can believe it, these swallows' ancestors were building nests on our big old pines at the time of the Resurrection, and maybe thousands of years before. So during the life of Christ, the Crusades, the fall of Rome, the black plague, the 100-year War, during Victoria's reign, World War II, the Korean War and right through 'Nam, our little feathered summer visitors were building nests, laying eggs, hatching chicks and flying south in the Fall, just exactly as they are doing today.

And that is only a 10th of a second in the realm of things, but doesn't seem to us poor mortals who fool ourselves, and convince ourselves how important the 20th century and its remaining years actually are. Horsefeathers! Only important to us because our ever-so-brief time happens to be now, in reality even putting it in blocks of one million years is sheer self-flattery.

John Talmadge at age 88 on 'Ace' in Rattlesnake Canyon, just east of the Rose Mine. Talmadge was taking part in a cattle drive from Big Bear down to the desert.

Chapter Thirty

ᏣᎥᏬ

Strange Home for Yellow Jackets

We were gathering cattle on the Oak Grove Ranch, to move them to Chihuahua Valley, when I stopped to observe a single large boulder near Temecula Creek that had 32 Indian grinding holes in it. Such a sight is spectacular evidence to the existence of aborigines who inhabited that waterway for hundreds and even thousands of years.

Dense chaparral extends in every direction from this location, with tall, tough red shank predominating, and gathering cattle was a chore in such country. About a mile further on, in passing the mouth of a wide, side canyon, there were to be seen about six or eight head of cattle in a little clearing, perhaps a quarter mile away. So pushing those already gathered to keep them moving in the right direction, I cut off up this side canyon and worked my way around behind these waywards and started them down toward the growing herd on the flat below. As this little bunch of eight head started downward, bawling and trotting, my attention was drawn to something very white, lying under a large bush, and upon investigation I found part of the bones of a large cow that had been dead for several years. Included was the complete skull with nice big cow horns still attached, and as such finds are not overly prevalent these days I decided to carry it down to the dirt road about a half mile away and come back for it in a pickup later that evening.

Because I was busy with the gathering chore it was necessary to hurry, so stepping off my horse I grabbed the skull by one horn, swung back on quickly and started to ride away. But it wasn't to be that easy! I discovered, within seconds, both myself and horse being attacked by numerous yellow jackets, and thinking the horse had stepped on and disturbed a nest of them, I kicked him out and ran away from the area. Pulling up a few hundred yards down the canyon I found the yellow jackets were still with us, more numerous than before and madder than ever. Fighting them off both myself and the horse, I looked at the cow skull I was carrying and was amazed to see the little flying torpedoes exiting in quick succession from the hollow part of the skull. The horse was about to buck me off and I had already taken a couple of blows (feels like a blow when yellow jackets sting). I picked out a thick low bush close-by and threw the skull into the top of it and got some quick distance between myself and the unusual hive they had chosen to inhabit. Killed a couple of persistent little pests, got my horse's head screwed back on straight and tied him up. Then I cut a long tree limb with small branches and leaves on the end, and walked back to where I could see the skull in the top of the bush where it had landed. At this point I prepared to do battle for possession of the contested skull. A home for them or a souvenir for me—but who said this world was fair.

However, there is little room for bragging rights in the ensuing war which eventually culminated in my having possession of the now safe and empty skull, but they did not give up readily as many of them sacrificed themselves to protect their home. Finally, after thrashing the skull with the tree limb, I grabbed the near empty prize and ran, fighting off the still-waring stingers with my branch, and at this point both I and the horse, whom I mounted, fired out of there *muy pronto*. We got a couple going-away stings, and still running a half-mile later there were yet a couple persistent, mad, suicidal yellow jackets dogging my retreat and determined to make their presence felt.

I still have the head mounted in the tack-room and as I think back on that little melee I marvel at the courage and persistence of those fiery yellow jackets. It is not to be denied, however, that hornets and bees have the same "don't tread on me" personalities, and if you 'parry' with them you do so at your own peril.

With that kind of a historical background this particular skull has become a "conversation piece" that piques the curiosity and interest of most people that spy it over the tackroom door. And the tale has been told and re-told on numerous occasions, without the aid of added deminsions and adjectives. It's certainly not an earth-shaking story, but I can feel those stings even now and vividly recall the occurrence every time it is mentioned, or when I notice the telltale skull above the door. Now that's some kind of pun folks—*telltale* skull!

Chapter Thirty-One

∾

Clark Gable Visits the I S Ranch

A 16-cylinder Packard convertible in 1932 was about 100 feet long, give or take a few feet. At least it looked that long parked in front of the ranch house on the Los Flores Talmadge Brothers cattle ranch, adjacent to present day Silverwood Lake.

No one there had ever seen a V-16, but upon going into the house we found ranch owner John Talmadge sitting in the front room having a conversation with an old friend, Gwen Baer, who ran an exclusive dude ranch in Apple Valley near Victorville. She had brought one of her ranch guests with her, Clark Gable himself, and therein lay the answer to the 16-cylinder Packard question.

After introductions and a short chat session, it became an obvious conclusion that everyone wanted to see and ride in the big car. As it turned out, Gable was very proud of the car and was obviously as eager to show it off as everyone was to test it. So after a couple short rides, and when everyone had looked under the hood at the engine—which was about the size of the one in PT 109—Gwen and Gable returned to Apple Valley. But that wasn't the last of Clark Gable we were to see!

Arrangements had been worked out for Gable to return the following week to go deer hunting on horseback and with a mounted guide from the ranch—who just so happened to be the author of this book. Deer season was open and the film star liked to hunt, and since the ranch owners, foreman and hands were all partial to both the fun of hunting and the taste of vension, it seemed like an advantageous arrangement to all concerned. This is to say nothing of the fact that there was certainly an allure to becoming hunting companions to Clark Gable, who at that time was cementing a fabulous career which was to last a quarter of a century.

He turned out to be very easy to know, a regular guy, savvy and ready for fun, hiking, hunting and swapping yarns. Everyone was surprised at how tall Gable was and how broad his shoulders—he practically had to duck and go sideways through the doors in that old ranch house.

When he returned by himself a week later, in the V-16 of course, he was happy to show everyone who was interested his matched pair of guns—a 12-gauge pump and a 30-06. They were very fancy, with gold and silver inlay and etchings of deer, ducks, elk, and geese. It was a very beautiful set, and he could hit a two-inch bulls-eye at a thousand yards with his scope-equipped 30-06. Not every time, but often.

His marksmanship proved he was a serious and successful shooter, but what did he do when a big buck jumped out in front of him and went crashing away in the brush? He didn't have time to do anything before the buck disappeared! Though we stayed around the area and tracked him for some time, we never did see the buck again.

The remainder of that memorable morning was spent with Gable and myself going up the toll road behind the Sawtooth Mountains and trying our hand at some hunting. That was a fairly steep, crooked, and narrow road in 1932, and he handled that big, long, convertible very expertly, though also fast and furiously, as he skidded or broadsided around each curve. He seemed to enjoy fast driving on borderline roads.

The tracks were there but the deer were not, and the hunters hiked several miles, then returned to the V-16 and were back at the ranch for lunch. We had good old Irish beef stew and Gable ate three helpings plus apple cobbler! Like I said, he was a big man.

Having seen nothing to shoot as yet, the decision was made to spend the afternoon hunting on horseback. The author saddled up "Chief" for Gable and "Chappo" for himself, and rode up through Cedar Springs and Cleghorn Canyon, and eventually up onto the top of Cleghorn on an old cow trail. Several deer and fawn were seen, but only one buck at a great distance, and he was going immediately out of sight over a ridge.

It might seem that the day was a total loss since upon our return to the ranch there hadn't been a shot fired, but that was not really the case. A beautiful, clear, crisp fall day, a pleasant morning hike in beautiful country, an afternoon horseback trip to the top of Cleghorn Mountain all added up to a very enjoyable day. Gable was enough of a hunter to realize that sometimes you get skunked, and so was satisfied, considering he had an outdoor day, good lunch, rode a good horse all afternoon at absolutely no cost to him, and was invited back any time by the ranchers, who enjoyed his company. At any rate his thanks and obvious appreciation were received by the ranch owners and foreman as sufficient payment.

Clark Gable had made a good, new and different type diversion for all on the ranch, and a topic of conversation every time another of his pictures came out—particularly so when "Gone With the Wind" was released. It seemed nice to personally know a man who was that professional at his chosen calling.

Chapter Thirty-Two

ᔕᖇ

Cowboy Ropes

Ropes—that word, to a cowboy, brings to mind a "lass" rope, a "piggin' string", "hard and fast", "dally", "two wraps and a hooey", "headin' and heelin' ", and "two hockin' em".

A rope on a ranch or rodeo, or as part of a cowboy's gear, is as important as any single item, since it is used for so many things. A hand on a cow-ranch, where there are acres per cow and not cows per acre, would no more saddle up a horse and even ride out to change the water or get the mail without a rope on his saddle. And if he is going after wild cattle, he will always carry two ropes, and rest assured he frequently and hopefully needs them both.

A "lass" rope is also known as a lasso and generally refers to any rope used by a cowboy to rope cattle or horses. Shorter lengths of preferably softer, and sometimes cotton rope are used to secure your horse for a few minutes, or sometimes all night in an overnight cow camp where there are no corrals, barns or horse facilities.

A much shorter, much smaller piece of rope is frequently carried on the saddle or even over the shoulder like a bandolier. This is known as a "piggin' string", and is used by rodeo hands to tie a calf's one front foot and two hind feet in a calf-roping event. This method is referred to as "two wraps and a hooey": first the loop end of the piggin' string is placed on one front foot; then two wraps are taken around that front foot and both hind feet; and finally, the "hooey", or half hitch, is placed around the two hind feet only, and pulled tight to keep the calf immobile as long as necessary. The judge then checks the tie and drops his flag to the timers, thus stopping the watch, and giving the roper the time he has earned. Twelve seconds or less is good, and 18 seconds or more is slow in today's rodeo competition.

However, the use of a piggin' string precedes the modern rodeo by many decades. It frequently was longer, softer, and stronger on a ranch hand's outfit. It was longer because it was used to tie down full grown stock part of the time, and softer, because instead of leaving it out for a few seconds, it might be on for several hours or even all night. While you didn't want the animal to escape, you also didn't want to cut off circulation for that length of time, because it might well cripple the beast. Also, it was stronger, because a 1500 pound bull could, by might and main, break a calf-sized piggin' string. The ranch hands often used the piggin' string to tie one front foot to the opposite side hind foot of wild cattle, with a little slack between. Then they could get to their feet and travel slowly, if at all. This is better for their general well-being than tying them down completely or even to tying them up, face to face, with a pine tree, pinon, or joshua.

"Hard and fast" refers to tying the end of your lass rope to the horn of the saddle. This is used mostly by rodeo calf-ropers. "Dally" occurs in rodeo team roping, or in general roping on a ranch, whether outside or in a corral, and consists of wrapping the end of the rope still in your possession around the horn of the saddle, counter-clockwise, after you have roped a cow or horse while on horseback.

There were more ropes on a ranch: ropes for a block and fall, ropes to pull the windmill, ropes to pull up the haystacker, ropes to pull up through the open front second story doors into the loft, ropes to tow stuck vehicles, wagons, and other equipment, ropes to hold around the remuda while the hands catch their horses, rope for a swing in the old cottonwood tree, heavy cotton rope to tie up a horse that is difficult to shoe, rope to head and tail a string of horses, rope for the Diamond Hitch, and at least one extra, not new, but usable lass rope in every vehicle on the ranch. There are so many kinds of and uses for rope on a ranch that some surely have been forgotten, but the foregoing will give the general idea.

It is interesting to note the different types, sizes and uses of rope to a cowhand or cattleman. You find 3/8 inch scant, 3/8 exact, or 3/8 full to 7/16 for lass ropes and hard, soft or medium lay; small, hard to medium soft for piggin' string, 1/2 inch cotton for best tie ropes, 3/4 to one inch cotton for shoeing a bad horse or tying one down to be doctored or cut. Lass ropes can be grass or nylon, and in Mexico they frequently use maguay ropes made of certain cactus fibers. In the Southwest and Mexico, the leather braided riata has always been favored by many cowboys, cowmen and vaqueros. Good using ropes for rodeo work now come in all colors, including: blue, gold, and even a combination red, white and blue are frequently seen being used by professional rodeo hands.

The length of the lass rope also varies greatly. "Hard and fast" calf ropes are sometimes as short as 24 feet, but John Talmadge made his own rawhide leather riatas which averaged out at about 65 feet. In rough country with big, wild cattle he often used it all. Of course, there are all lengths in between these two examples. John always said that there are two kinds of cowboys who don't "dally", those that don't know how and those that are afraid to. When he was roping those big old white-faced mother cows on the IS, I have seen him let about two yards of rope slip around the horn to keep from jerking one of those old cows, and a thin spiral of smoke would rise up from the horn—he wasn't about to "chouse" one of those good old range cows any more than he could help, and if you expected to continue to work there, you'd better not, either.

We might mention "hondos", the little enclosed circle at one end of a lass rope that forms the loop, and which the rest of the rope "ran through". Some were tied with a very simple granny knot with the end run through it and pulled down tight. Some leather hondos for riatas were solid leather 3/4 inch thick and complicated, hard to make, but lasted the life-time of the rope, and the rope flowed smoothly and freely through it, never becoming bound or caught.

Some hondos of grass, nylon, or maguay had a leather or rawhide "burner" on the end of the loop of the hondo itself to keep the hondo from wearing. There are also metal hondos and wire hondo burners. Almost any rope used on a ranch for any purpose will have a hondo in one end—it just makes 'em handier for *almost* any purpose. Even sisel ropes were sometimes used for mundane, non-critical purposes on a ranch because, if it could be used, it was cheaper. So, there were many kinds of hondos. Most were satisfactory, and their only real jobs were to "balance the loop" and "run free".

This description of ropes has been written from the angle of a cow ranch, rodeo, and cowboys (and girls). No attempt has been made to try to explain "rope" as used by ships and sailors, though they are also of extreme importance to that calling. Anyway, I could never get used to calling it "cable" or "wire", or whatever seagoing folk say. Outside of ranching, the many uses and abuses of rope by people over thousands of years have given it many meanings and connotations. In different parts of the world it is called by other names: in Africa, Oxneim; in Falconny, brail; in Scotland, whang; in the U.S., tackle, hangman's rope, noose, necktie. We have adages and descriptions, such as: "give him enough rope and he will hang himself" and "rope of sand", as well as words to say what a rope does: hog tie, make fast, tether, frontfoot, heel, hobble, picket, catch, snare, and even "rope"!

I can't imagine the West without ropes, and in the Old West many a cattle rustler or horse thief was hanged with his own lass rope, taken off his saddle, and used on the nearest big old cottonwood tree that the posse or vigilantes could find. You have to admit that quick justice is certainly a deterrent, but I just hope they didn't make too many mistakes. Anyway, with that kind of justice, recidivism went way down.

The author at age 17 on 'Eleck' leading 'Chappo' en-route to "Squints" for a few days of gathering wild cattle with the Hitchcock Ranch hands.

Early "Hairy" Days of Search & Rescue

When the sheriff's substation at Big Bear came into being—just after World War II—it was in total charge of search and rescue, and Emmett L. Shay was then Sheriff of San Bernardino County. However, the fire departments, the constable, the Forest Service and private citizens were quick to help when needed, and without them this two-man (and sometimes only one-man) substation would have been iced.

Those early years did offer some good, bad, hairy, scary, dangerous and nearly impossible tasks to perform. And initially it did so without posses, radio communications, scuba divers, helicopters or any other specialized equipment now taken for granted. Dr. Godwin's airplane, a couple Jeeps and one "Weasel" was the extent of special equipment. What did it have? Rope, civilian horsemen and their mounts, the best trackers in the Southwest, enthusiasm, youth and a lot of outdoor expertise.

During the 1940's and 50's, the present equipment slowly evolved. One item after another was begged, borrowed, stolen and even occasionally acquired as a budget item. To begin with, there were grappling hooks that John Talmadge made in 1909, which were initially used to help recover the bodies of Oat and Willy Talmadge, sons of William Talmadge, who drowned in Papoose Bay. The bodies were not found for weeks, and were eventually located only after a deep sea diver was brought up from San Pedro.

When the need was brought to their attention, local businessmen almost without exception were very generous in supplying ropes and other useful items. Such grappling hooks and throwing ropes, and boats borrowed at one time or another from every boat landing on the lake came in very handy, because every year of that period from one to eight persons drowned in the lake each summer.

At one time in the early 50's there were five persons drowned in the east end of the lake one afternoon, all out of the same speeding inboard that turned turtle on a fast maneuver and sank almost at once. Luckily, we had them all out by dark, but all by grappling hook, as there were no scuba divers in the area and it was no use calling down the hill. All the searchers had was a little rowboat with a small piece of glass in the bottom, a "glass-bottom boat" that worked well then and on other occasions here, as well as the Colorado River, Lake Arrowhead and elsewhere. When you got that boat you got Deputy Al Oehl, and he squeezed more good, professional mileage and good public relations out of that questionable piece of equipment than you can shake a stick at. He was the kind of a deputy no sheriff's office ever has enough of, and his talents went far beyond search and rescue.

On another occasion in the late 1940's or early 50's, a couple of persons in a little two-tailed safety type airplane were buzzing fishermen in boats in the area near the dam. Finally, and foreseeably, on their 10th pass or so they augured into about 40 feet of water. Some job—a whole airplane and two men on the bottom—with no equipment for properly handling it and no one who had ever been involved in such an endeavor. By that time private citizens knew they were welcome to help, and a dozen locals and a borrowed fishing scow, flat bottomed and stable, was, along with the deputies, out on the lake with the aforementioned old grappling hooks, attempting to locate and hook onto the plane, and that was at the very end of the too short throw ropes.

When they did hook on and, with great difficulty and might and main, pulled it to the surface, it will always be remembered that Bruce Munro, the postmaster, took charge, and under his orders the airplane was successfully raised. This is just one example of local help and enthusiasm. We then had to extricate the bodies, and they—having gone into the water right behind the hot engine—were cooked red, and the flesh came off easily and made that job most difficult. The whole idea of local help never came in more handily. When the sheriff's office had no money and few men, the citizens always took up the slack.

Sometime in the early 1950's a call was received by the local substation, and immediate response was sent to Hanna Flats campground north of Fawnskin where a four-year-old boy was reported lost. As luck so often has it, the parents searched for several hours until almost dark before calling the sheriff. This made the sheriff's job a difficult one, that of tracking a very small boy in total, moonless darkness. So with three men carrying flashlights and extra batteries—two of them deputies and the third a professional local tracker, George Birdsell—a big circle was cast around the camp. Located within 30 minutes was what appeared to be the boy's track (the right size, and fresh) going down a well-used trail directly west of the camp. After tracking for almost a mile, now going down a canyon, something popped up that put everyone's heart in their throats—a good-sized bear track was also going down the trail, fresh and on top of the little boy's tracks.

Now bear in these mountains were not dangerous to people, and I don't recall when a person was so injured. All involved had repeatedly told the public and local and visiting citizens that the bear were not dangerous. However, this situation put all of those of that faith to the test, and frankly no one right then was so all-fired sure that the little boy was all that safe.

We sweated the situation for the next half mile, hurrying down the canyon trail, when, much to our relief, the bear track turned off and went up a little side canyon while the boy's little paddle marks went on down the main trail. The boy still had not been found, the night was getting cold, and the parents were presumed to be beside themselves, but those on the trail breathed a sigh of relief, and the walking and tracking now seemed like a lark and a cinch to turn out OK. And, sure enough, a little farther down, the boy was found asleep under a bush alongside the trail. With dirty hands and tear-stained face, he looked like a tired, pooped-out little angel.

We woke the boy, calmed him down in the face of so many strangers, and carrying him, started back up the trail to the campgrounds and his parents and brothers and sisters. Shortly, and expecting an excited and thankful pair of parents, the boy was taken to the tent, whereupon the father partly opened the door flap, called the boy in and shut the flap, period. No appreciation shown, no thank-you, no nothing. After standing around shifting from one foot to the other, and embarrassed by the parents' attitude, the search group then wandered off to their cars and went home.

Once again we realized that the two deputies, the special deputies, and volunteers could almost always handle any problem, and we all were exceedingly proud of that reputation. Only infrequently was it necessary to ask for assistance from the main office in San Bernardino. Besides, the main office didn't have any specially trained men, and Big Bear probably had more cold weather and snow-rescue type equipment that they. Even though almost all of it was privately owned, it was placed at the substation's disposal any time and instantly, and probably the owner came with it.

In 1946 and 1947, by the skin of our teeth, several emergencies were handled successfully to everyone's satisfaction, with no bad publicity or scenes or dissatisfied customers. In 1948 the first San Bernardino Mountain Posse was formed, consisting of 25 horsemen, trucks and trailers, and 500 feet of rope. Dr. Godwin served as surgeon and pilot, in his own plane, and at his own expense. There were many successful searches for lost persons, injured hunters and fishermen, downed airplanes, snowbound miners and overdue skiers and hikers. This substation at this time was issued the first four-wheel-drive vehicle ever in the San Bernardino County Sheriff's office. Afterwards, we wondered how we had ever existed without it.

About 1950, the substation commander gave a talk to the Lions Club and explained the lack of search and rescue equipment. They, on the spot, voted to make the acquisition of a trailer and many pieces of equipment their yearly project. We now had Sutherland's Weasel, also at his time and expense, and Jim Hendricks made us an emergency-type Toboggan with a curl at either end, and donated it to the posse. And "Doc" Pardee, local druggist, donated a large first aid kit and some snakebite kits. Two-way civilian radios in privately owned Jeeps now also came into use at their owners' expense and time. (How did we do without them?)

Times have changed, and Big Bear is no longer a little village. People also change, and the county and the sheriff's office grow with the great influx of people and money. But beyond any doubt, the time, gasoline and equipment noted in preceding paragraphs would cost the taxpayers a half-million dollars in this decade. Maybe even more—what does a chopper cost these days?

The state of the art now is: scuba divers, special enforcement details, SWAT, helicopters, airplanes, trained mountain rescuers, mobile and airborne communications centers, paramedics, infra-red cameras and gun sights, four-wheel-drive rescue vehicles, and all this a part and parcel of the best sheriff's office in the Southwest. People who live here are so close to the forest they sometimes cannot see the trees, but they should be very proud of what their tax dollars are accomplishing for them in the San Bernardino County Sheriff's Office.

Chapter Thirty-Four

ᕳᐤ

Monte Was Not a Card Game

Bud Waite and Monte—a good, part-Indian cowboy, and a good high-strung cow-horse. They made quite a pair.

Bud was an all-around ranch cowboy; had been one all his life. He was also a horse-breaker of considerable reputation and a rodeo bronc rider. And Monte was fast, well-trained, smart, good at handling, driving and roping cattle but skittish, high-strung, unpredictable in some instances and very predictable in others.

An M.D. in Banning owned Monte and hired Bud to break him, which he did. During the following spring the doctor was riding Monte on a Talmadge Brothers roundup and drive to Big Bear. Just below the Needle's Eye in Rattlesnake Canyon something frightened the little horse and the doctor (who was not a horseman) pulled Monte over on top of him in a big rock pile. The doctor's back was broken. He had to be carried over a mile to Rose Mine and taken to a hospital where he almost died. He was in the hospital for months and at that time gave Monte to Bud.

For his entire life Monte was very touchy. If a rattlesnake sang close or a butterfly, bird or quail flew out from under his nose, he would buck hard and high for at least a hundred yards. He wasn't fooling and he wasn't crow-hopping. I think he honed Bud's bronc-riding ability, and was at least part of the cause of Bud's many first prizes in rodeo saddle bronc riding down through the years.

Bud was raised on the reservation and learned to shoot, ride and track very readily and professionally even as a teenager. Then he went to work for various cow ranches for the next many years, using his riding and tracking abilities to the fullest extent.

A traumatic experience occurred about the time Bud was given Monte. It happened at Warren's Well in Yucca Valley. One morning Monte threw one of his fits at the barn with only Bud's saddle on and he bucked around the yard and up behind the house to the barbed

131

wire fence than ran east and west there. He turned with the fence, placed his shoulder against the barbed wire and continued to buck and press for over 100 feet, tearing his shoulder open badly, clean to the bone. Most horsemen (including the author) would have put the horse down and out of his misery, but Bud had some sentimental attachment as well as great respect for the little sorrel. He sewed his shoulder up, and doctored and cared for him for months. Although a large scar was always thereafter noticeable, the horse went on punching cows, bucking and being his individual self for many years.

He never was gentle broke, and I don't think Bud would have felt about him as he did if the little horse had ever gotten dog gentle.

Bringing a little bunch into Shay's Corral to work the cattle, i.e., brand calves, doctor cows, cut off bad ingrown horns, etc.

ᴄᴏᴏ

Tools of the Trade

Undoubtedly, every job, profession, occupation and endeavor has certain tools necessary to its exact needs. The carpenter needs a hammer and saw; the doctor needs a stethescope and thermometer; the mason needs a level and a trowel and so on, through all the world-wide thousands of jobs being done in a million areas. The "tools of the trade" are included in the "way of life" of a cattle rancher and his hired cowpunchers. Some of their tools seem different, but almost all of them are used by some other professions for similar type jobs. But the cowboy, the vaquero, the gaucho, and others whose main occupation is "the care of bovine animals while mounted on equine animals", use tools which are very similar or exactly the same, in almost all instances. An item may be different looking in Australia, but its purpose and function will be the same as that used by the Argentine gaucho.

The "trade" is the production of beef for the tables of the world. The "tools" are many and varied, and certain subtle differences can even be distinguished between areas as close as Montana and Texas. Sometimes slight but distinguishable differences can even be seen on neighboring ranches.

The controversial items? Length of ropes, single or double rig; snaffle bit vs. hackamore; humane mouthpiece vs. spade bit; form fitter vs. flat; tied reins with romal, as compared to separate reins; walking vs. undershot heels; ox bow vs. wide stirrups; square vs. round skirts; batwing vs. shotgun vs. chino; long shank vs. short shank; Chihuahua rowels vs. small many-pointed rowels; narrow brim vs. broad; high crown vs. low; felt vs. straw; Levi's vs. Lees; split ear vs. throat latch; Tapaderos vs. open stirrups; silver vs. plain; cotton rope strand vs. inner tube section; and more.

So, what is the required gear for a buckaroo, a gaucho, or a vaquero? There are many varieties and prejudices in every item to be discussed.

When you realize you are talking about men (and women) on a least three or four continents, each beef industry developing almost wholly on its own, it is not surprising that their tools can be, and in some instances are, widely divergent.

The most basic item perhaps is the saddle, and the differences can be seen to be widely biforcated—almost no similarities. But one thing can be noted, they all are made for heavy use, and designed to be comfortable for both the horse and the rider, during long, hard hours of work. The American cowboy and the vaqueros of Mexico have a saddle horn which one way or another are used to secure ropes after latching on to a critter. The Argentine gaucho and the Australian cattle station employee have no saddle horn, but do rope and get the job done in their own ways. The stirrup and stirrup leathers of the American range rider and the Australian out-back rider do not even resemble one another. Bits and headstalls too are dissimilar, but each area or continent in their own way have come up with that type of equipment that best stops, turns and backs their mounts to their satisfaction, and gets the job done with their type horses, cattle and terrain.

Hats really have only one thing in common—they all have broad enough brims to keep the sun off, from the 2½ inch Stetson to over a foot for Mexican sombreros. Boots may be an item where all agree as closely as on any piece of equipment. They're all made to protect the lower leg and to be comfortable in the stirrups, but here we do find a wide open area in the case of heels, from sharply pointed three-inch (or higher) undershot heels to flat walking heels.

Other areas of actual riding gear are also in question and not universally agreed upon—but there are areas other than horse gear where "tools of the trade" can also be apropos to the working stockman. Such an item is fence-pliers, a specialty tool, which most use in mundane, routine, fence building or fence mending chores. But some waddies get real fancy and professional with this fencing item and make them accomplish things which even their manufacturer does not know they are capable of, such as fancy corners, drum tight supports, and formidable gates. These gates are strong, yet easy to open and close, and adhering to the old formula that the gate must be stronger than the fence.

Such mundane tools as shovels, picks, bars, wrenches, screwdrivers, hammers, pliers don't sound particularly Western or romantic—and they are not, but every rancher and cowboy is very familiar with their uses. Cattle squeezes, windmills, trucks, trailers, and so on, must all be repaired, and you can't do it with a "lass rope", a "piggin' string", spurs, or a big hat.

No cowboy ever worked on the author's or any neighboring ranch who did not shoe his own horses, and sometimes a few on the side to make a little extra cash. The author shod his first horse when he was 13, and his grandfather was still shoeing horses well up into his 80's. So we find shoeing tools, anvils, nails, and forges, among the more important items of ranch gear; the San Bernardino Mountains and the Mojave Desert, by and large, are too rough and rocky to ride barefooted horses.

I only knew of one horse who never was shod, never needed to be, and never went lame. This horse, whose name was "Nevada", ran with a semi-wild bunch that ranged from Warren's Well in Yucca Valley to Upper and Lower Covington Flats, Smith Canyon, and the Eureka Peak area. He was so damn mean that he was only caught once or twice a year at round-up when we always needed extra horses. Was he a handful!—an eleven hundred pound bay, capable of kicking, biting, bucking, and running away. No dudes, and not all the cowboys, could ride him. He was a challenge, but if you took Nevada as your extra horse and rode him for a month and held up your end of the work, you were a cowboy and had something to be proud of.

Nevada was hard to catch, hard to saddle and probably would buck every morning and any other time he felt you loose or off-balance in the saddle. But if you could ride him he was fast and savvy, especially agile and athletic in rough country. He handled his end of roping very well, cut cattle well, traveled easily and tirelessly, and of course never went lame, never got sick, never was shod, and took care of himself the rest of the year running with the wild bunch. Finally, he went loco one Fall about 1940 and the author was forced to shoot him in a little canyon just north of Eureka Peak. (Excuse me, "put him down").

Nevada, now that horse brings back several memories—he was famous in his time, or maybe I should say notorious, because though lots or horses were as good a cowhorse as he, very few stayed that mean and ornery for 18 years or more. But one day, about 1938, my granddad, on Ace, myself on Eleck and Frank Urton on Nevada were driving a little bunch of cattle from Morongo Valley to Warren's Well. We were approaching the dry lake at the west end of the valley, and the cattle boogered from something and ran sharply to the right. Frank and Nevada were walking on that side, and because of the acceleration of the cattle, he had to kick Nevada into a quick lope and try to turn them. Well, although both we and the horses had had a full day riding, Nevada felt Frank loose in the saddle, and tired or not, he let him down, bucked at least one hundred yards and darn near got him off. There was lots of daylight between Frank and his saddle on several jumps, but he rode him pretty, though shook up. Finally, when he got him stopped, Nevada was bleeding from the mouth and nose. Nevada was a teen-aged horse by that time. Anyway, I put Eleck into a run and headed the cattle back in the right direction. (The dry lake bed referred to is now Yucca Valley's Blue Skies Golf Course).

And that, for sure, is another of the "tools of the trade"—a cow-boy's horse. As can be shown, they ranged from fairly small to quite large (1300 pounds), from gentle and helpful partners in the business to Nevada and his ilk. Every ranch had a few of the rank ones, and the horses, all of them at one time or another, were the topic of conversation around the evening campfire. Listening to those stories of good ones, bad ones, fast ones, and some of the things they did that were exceptional, some of the wild runs, some of the spectacular falls, and stories of getting your head stuck in the dirt, all combined to make life-long impressions on young boys and young cowboys which they would remember and re-tell to their own grandkids. 'Course by the time they were telling them to their young 'uns, they were the heros of the tales—but what the heck, that's what story telling is all about.

Almost hate to end it this way, but it must be acknowledged that modern ranches also include as "tools of the trade" such items as trucks and trailers, tractors, back-hoes, pick-ups and cattle squeezes. Even airplanes and helicopters are now used to find cattle, drive cattle, count cattle, drop salt where needed, drop hay in emergencies, and quickly look over the range after a heavy rain or snow to see if any cattle are in trouble. They can be, and are also used, to patrol, find rustlers and assist in arrests.

The definition and description of "tools" still include all of the old ones on a working cow ranch, but have to admit that the new, exotic ones certainly change the picture in many ways of today's beef industry. In some ways, it is an improvement (though an expensive one) to be able to drop hay to cattle in deep snow, many of whom would die except for that assistance. That old mother cow looks up, and sees a bale of hay falling. She pushes her way through drifts of snow to get to it, takes her big calf with her, watches it start to eat the first food in a week, and takes a big bite for herself. She looks up, and you can almost hear her thanks when she tells her hungry, almost starving calf, "who said there is no God?"

The production of food is very underrated in this time, and farmers are looked down upon as somehow inferior and less smart than a resident of New York City, for example. This is not true of course, and *no* thinking person really believes that. The beef rancher is in the same category, and though he has a romantic history, what modern man is apt to forget—because of the abundance of food, chain grocery stores, fruit and vegetables so abundant, meat of all types at his fingertips—is the following philosophical truth: "Civilization was, is, and always will be based on the food supply."

Thus, the farmer and stock raiser are actually the backbone of society and in reality are the pillars upon which civilization is built. This is more than can be said for the manufacturers of automobiles, real estate agents, telephone linemen, even kings and presidents!

Tools of the Trade: 30-30 rifle, spade bit, branding iron, 45 calibre six-shooter, lass rope, saddle, spurs, saddle blanket.

Bear Valley Cowboys Were a Breed Apart

The Hitchcock and Myzelle (Y double H) Ranch used Holcomb Valley as its summer range and actually owned several thousand acres of it. The summer range also included Hunsucker Flat (now Running Springs), Allison Ranch (the old Heap Ranch), Big Pine Flats, Coxey Ranger Station Meadow, Cienega Largo, Cienega Redondo, Green Valley and Crabbe Flats, as well as Mud Springs, the Old Sheep Corral, Lion Canyon and Squint's Ranch. In the winter they ran their cattle in what is now Apple Valley, also at Grapevine, Isabella and Oak Springs, as well as the Bowen Ranch area.

Will Hitchcock, the old man; Bob Hitchcock, the son; and Bob Hitchcock, the grandson, did much of their own cowboying, along with Bill Myzelle, who had married Gladys Hitchcock and became a working partner in the ranch. But they did hire and use such good cowhands as Bob Reed, Slim Spence, Homer Urton, Jim Dever and Mart McGinnis. Actually, a book could be written about either Jim Dever or Homer Urton; their fame at what they did spread far and wide. Like Dan Fouts in football or Sandy Koufax in baseball, Dever and Urton stood out from the rest as superior cow punchers. It is unfortunate they are not included in the Cowboy Hall of Fame, but it seems that only the big names of the professional rodeo circuits and other highly acclaimed positions make it there.

This too was a rough-country, hard-riding outfit, and always had many wild cows, steers and orahana (unmarked and unbranded) bulls to handle. These were roped, tied down, and led out either from horseback or by driving them out with some gentle cattle. The latter was accomplished by putting a toggle which was a Y shaped oak branch, or a chain on one front foot.

In their back country, Largo, Squint's and White Mountain, there were always some old, wise, runaway steers six or nine or even 12 years old. And they are what made cowboys work for $30 a month

138

and found (room and board): the wildest adventure that 999 men out of 1000 ever had is pale and tame and unexciting in comparison to tracking down, running and roping, tying down or tying up, leading or driving out of the mountains those big old steers.

With no exaggeration, I can say I saw several steers from the Y double H or the Los Flores whose withers were the same height as a 16-hand horse. They were hard to catch because their stride in rocks, brush and steep country was equal to a horse's stride, and they knew every rock, tree, bush and side trail in their home range, which probably covered 100 square miles. Add to this the fact that they had been run several times and had gotten away, and were much wilder and alert than the deer they ran with.

Almost without exception, all you heard or knew was a rustle in the brush or a rolling rock way ahead of you when they saw or heard the horses' metal shoes biting rock, or even a man's whisper 250 yards away. All that would be there when you arrived would be a thin string of s--t, and from there you tracked and ran 'til you caught up, sometimes four or five miles—and sometimes you never did.

A rough outfit, ask anyone, but Bob Hitchcock, Sr., was cowboy enough, man enough and ramrod enough to get the job done and did so for over 40 years. *Un macho homo sapien.*

One reason the Hitchcock ranch could function in that country was because they were never without good and mostly big, well-broke cowhorses. Some outstanding examples were Spike, Snip, Mose, Baldy, Traveler, Bay Larry, Gouella, Mickey, Pony and Midget. Midget was a little horse because Homer Urton liked them short and easy to mount, but Pony, used a lot in rough country by Mart McGinnis, was a tall, long-legged horse and a bear in rough country.

Bob Hitchcock Sr., told me the best horse he ever rode was Snip, out of a work mare and a little stud later cut and used on the ranch for 20 years, named Baldy. Bob said in all the years he rode Snip in that kind of country, the horse never tripped or stumbled—a mighty record when you know the country and the cattle he faced. Bob Hitchcock Jr., told me the best horse he ever rode had to be Bay Larry, who excelled in all ways, more than most horses at any one thing.

The location of the four ranches I have written about—their owners, their cowhands, histories, tales, yarns, horses and cattle are well established.

Big Bear, Baldwin, Big Meadows and Holcomb Valley all had the well-known mountain meadows famous for their rich, fast-fattening properties. Cattle on the 7,000 foot elevation grazing put on weight nearly as rapidly as they do in a feed lot, only the meat had a lot more flavor.

The present residents of the San Bernardino Mountains, by and large are unaware of their former neighbors, and are indeed hard-pressed to visualize cattle running wild and loose where now we have houses, paved roads, lawns, flowers, cement drives and blacktop parking lots, Col. Sanders and his Kentucky chickens, supermarkets, and other unmistakable signs of "progress".

The ranches we have been displaying were all large, and it is hard to visualize a local ranch of 750,000 acres, but that was the size of the IS Ranch in its heyday.

Cattlemen are good neighbors, and in Big Bear, for instance, the IS Ranch built the road down Red Ant Hill when finances kept the county from doing so. The Ranch also donated a fair-sized piece of land near the old IS barn at Metcalf Bay, signing it over to the county for the building of a road, at no cost to the county. Also, and this was an annual contribution, every Fourth of July the IS furnished for the community picnic a full-grown 1,000-pound beef, which Will Talmadge killed, dressed out, then dug the B-B-Q pit, wrapped the meat, hauled the wood, cooked the meat and helped serve—all this every year, for many years. All the proceeds went to the Chamber of Commerce, the Women's Club, etc.—Yup, the Talmadges' didn't make any money doing all this, but they did create a backlog of goodwill and comradeship with their friends and neighbors.

The ranch horses from all four ranches that have been discussed were unique and special, each particularly adept at their profession. They were mostly ranch bred and raised. Most were cold-blooded with maybe a little thoroughbred, Arab, Morgan, quarter or saddle-bred blood. All, however, are remembered by those who punched cows on them because they were tough, rugged, mountain-wise, desert-smart and rough-country acclimated. These were the horses of which it was said, "The country all looks level to them," a sincere and had-to-be-earned compliment. Many horses, of course, did not come up to that standard, and hundreds were sold or traded to replace them with horses that could stand up to the work they were asked to do. A horse with no "bottom" (stamina) or "wind" (lung capacity) or athletic ability was soon gone. Those that stayed had what we referred to as "cow-sense". Some had it, some didn't.

The present day fancy dinner houses have never served, even for

$20 to $30 per plate, anything to equal beefsteak, potatoes and gravy, beans, Dutch oven biscuits, coffee and canned peaches for dessert; that is really hard to beat. 'Course, maybe it tasted extra good because we hadn't eaten since 4:30 a.m., and it was now growing dark. It was an adventuresome, exciting and demanding outdoor man's existence. If only the youth of today were kept as busy as the youngsters in those days, doing something constructive, challenging, dangerous, rewarding, and fun: riding eight to 12 hours per day, punching cows, branding calves, sleeping outdoors on the ground and learning to shoe, break and train horses, doctor cattle, build fence, open springs, repair windmills, irrigate mountain pastures. Going to the occasional picnic, dance, family reunion, birthday and anniversary celebrations, and punkin' rollin' (small, local rodeos), were all twice as much fun as standing around on street corners and "cruising".

Seems that people are so sated with drinking, smoking, sex, wild parties, wife swapping, pot, dope, strikes, abortions (pro and con), the national debt, South Africa, Save the Whales, etc., that there is little time left for living, enjoying life and loving thy neighbor, even if he is of another faith, another color, another inclination, another political party; seems we could learn a lot from the pioneers in general and those of the San Bernardino Mountains in particular (because we know many of them in a personal way). Did they live simple lives? Yes. Boring lives? No. Fulfilling lives? Yes. Selfish lives? No. Happy lives? Yes. Maybe we could well compare that with our own lives in the supposedly advanced society of the latter 20th Century.

The stories, tales, far-fetched truths and homespun philosophies that are conjured up by the act of writing down the men's names, horses' names and place names are memories of a former time, now long gone. It was a wonderful time in the history of Big Bear Valley. When you look over the hard work, simple pleasures and early sunrises, you realize it was not a job or an occupation nor a profession—it was "a way of life".

finis